From A to BIBA

From A to BIBA
The Autobiography
of Barbara Hulanicki

V&A Publishing

First published by Hutchinson & Co. Ltd, 1983
This edition first published by V&A Publications, 2007
V&A Publishing
Victoria and Albert Museum
South Kensington
London SW7 2RL
www.vandapublishing.com

Distributed in North America by
Harry N. Abrams, Inc., New York

ISBN-13 978 1 85177 514 9
Library of Congress Control Number 2006936578
10 9 8 7 6 5 4
2014 2013 2012

A catalogue record for this book is available from the
British Library.

Cover design by V&A Design
Front cover photograph: © Neil Libbert, 1969
Back cover illustration: Biba Postal Boutique, drawing by Barbara
Hulanicki, 1964
Inside front and back cover illustrations: © Barbara Hulanicki
Page 182 illustration: Kasia Charko, V&A: AAD-1996/6/4

Printed in Great Britain by CPI Group (UK) Ltd, Croydon, CR0 4YY

V&A Publishing

Supporting the world's leading
museum of art and design,
the Victoria and Albert
Museum, London

To All Optimists, Fatalists and Dreamers

Acknowledgements

My thanks go to Professor J. Szuldrzynski, Leonard Hankin, Vincent Fitz-Simon, Gertrude Fitz-Simon, Elizabeth Fitz-Simon, Molly Parkin, Cathy McGowan, Frankie McGowan, Cilla Black, Bobby Willis, Mr and Mrs John Hunt, Eddy Hunt, Norma Moriceau, Mr and Mrs George Dingemans, Rosie and Tony Bartlett, Georgie Robbins, Patrick Hughes, Alan Siegel, John Ling, Mr and Mrs Andrew Goodman, Bob Pegner, Mr Skelly, Terry Apsey, John Grasemark, Peter Church, Jackie Modlinger, David Mainey, Leslie Lake, Marit Allen, Sandy Lieberson, Uriah, Tim Whitmore, Deidre McSharry, Anne Chubb, Michael Wright, Youni and Hiroshi Kurihara, the Kobayashi Family, Leslie Russell, Leonard, Patricia Lamburn, Ernestine Carter, Bridget Keenan, Jean Dobson, Felicity Green, Alan Farmer, Ian Farmer, Wally Rose, Sidney Riseman, Manny Davies, Andrew Logan, Michael Davis, Peter and Richard Logan, Robert and Sandy Lacey, Marco Nanini, Edgar Gurgel Aranha, Rita Lee, Antonio Bevar, Nally Bellati, Manfredi Bellati, Mick Rock, Tim Street-Porter, Aina, Gunda, Regis Houet, Desmond O'Neil, Anthony Little, Diana Walsh, Mrs Dearing, James Wedge, Helmut Newton, Hans Feurer, Harry Peccanotti, Sarah Moon, Rolph Gobbits, Elio Fiorucci, Christina Fiorucci, Orlando, Janet Street-Porter, Jay Musson, Del Howard, Mr Murray, Gay Burdett, Vanessa Gregory, Kim Willot, Elenor Powell, Irene Stasturshka, Freda McLare, Lois Hamilton, Marek Jaroszewicz, Aniela Mieczyslawska, Count Raczynski, Waclew Milewski, Tadeusz Piszcozkowski, David and Liz Smith, John McConnell, Sarah Plunket, Elizabeth Dickson, Anne Ryan, Mary Neal, Shirley Lowe, Teresa Ritchie, Joanne Brogden, Courtney Jones, Beatrix Miller, Prudence Glynn, Jane Bacon, Twiggy, Jenny Peel, Joe Dingemans, Lilly Anderson, Maureen Williamson, Claude Brouet, Constanza Pascalotti, Dougie Fields, Frank Citanovitch, Tony Elliott, Bevis Hillier, Ingrid, Doreen Spooner, Kasia Charko, Sir Hugh Fraser, Geoffrey Hill, Philip Norman, Michael Rand, Serena Sinclair, Katherine Hadley, all ex-Biba girls, waiters and cooks and Susan Hill.

Foreword

I hope you enjoy this period piece. Savour some of the fun and the fast pace we all lived in. The sixties was a giddy time, fuelled by energy generated from the release of new ideas and freedom of thought after the depressing, stifling post-war years. Biba burst from this background as a rebellious free spirit. I am always asked, who did the marketing? It was all Fitz, my husband, Stephen Fitz-Simon. Fitz shepherded and harnessed the rolling ball of energy. He picked it up and ran with it. He used to call me the golden goose. Business life then was spontaneous, lived from day to day, untouched by corporate rules. Everyone in Biba worked hard. There were no passengers. Drones were wholeheartedly rejected by the girls in the shop. Biba was the first feminist company. Only Fitz could keep up with the disciplined energy generated by women working together. No need for fancy offices, boardrooms or endless meetings producing no results. There was no time for that. The shop up front was the show, the beautiful shop girls who worked the front becoming more gorgeous by the hour. At the back of the house was the hard grind to produce new product, colours and decor to satisfy the hungry customers. It was always a strong family team that moved the whole business forward, with Fitz at the helm.

For twelve years, Fitz and I never ventured outside the four walls of Biba. After Big Biba closed, Fitz and I were able to get our private life back on track with our son, Witold, and the three of us became a family again. There was a wondrous but frightening world outside. Bruised, we left England to lick our wounds in private and start a new life.

After all these years it is wonderful to see how so many people have held on to their Biba dresses and how other products have found such memories. How satisfying to know that all those dresses never fell apart, as was always alleged they would at the time, and what a thrill to see them fetching such exorbitant prices at auctions and on eBay. Most gratifying, however, is to see the passion and the devotion still harboured by the Biba Babies, who grew up having tea on the toadstools in the roof garden while Alice in Wonderland made the tea. The objects have become more than just gorgeous things. They have become souvenirs of a special time to show their children. Today the Biba Babies tell me how we changed their lives. Fitz would have been so thrilled to hear that.

Thank you all for being such great patrons. Our genuine love and affection for the public has been reciprocated over and over again, year after year. It was a great and unique era that ended when Fitz died nine years ago. It fills me with so much joy that it has been kept alive in the hearts and imaginations of so many and now in a new edition of this book. I would once again like to thank Susan Hill who tortured me to get it finished, and Tim Whitmore, who both died some years ago. Thank you Susan for your dedication and thank you Tim for the wonderful work on the Big Biba.

Barbara Hulanicki

2007

Chapter One

I was brought up in Palestine, a land where it seemed to be eternally sunny. My childhood was so secure that I remember wishing one of my parents would die so I could feel some emotion, even misery. I was twelve years old when my wish came true.

It was February 1948 and we were in Jerusalem. I was lying awake at dawn, which was unusual for me. The house was quiet but in a far-away bedroom I could hear my father get up and start to dress. He must have sensed what was about to happen. The evening before, he had given me the fountain pen he always used, a very strange thing for him to have done.

At about six in the morning there was a bang on the front door. My father, whose name was Witold, went to answer it. Words were exchanged, he went back to his bedroom. I heard my mother putting on her dressing gown, whispers, then exclamations of panic. He was in a hurry to leave. I realize now that he wanted to go quickly to lead the danger away from the nest.

On his way out he popped his head round the door to take a look at his three children: myself, Beatrice, then ten, and my youngest sister, Biba. He saw I was awake and said, 'Basia, look after your mother – goodbye.' I didn't jump out of bed and kiss and hug him, I just let him go. It has always haunted me that I didn't reach out to touch him for the last time.

It should have been a normal grumpy morning. My father used to wake me early and I'd do exercises with him because I was porky and his muscles were turning to flab. In my usual half sleepy doze I would go through the routine of waving my arms and legs around while he lectured me about being fat. After the jerks, we would sit down and have a massive breakfast of cream cheese, butter and poppy seed bread, and I never lost any weight.

That morning my mother, Victoria, had dressed hastily. I became aware of another person in the house, got up and went to the hall. There was a giant of a man leaning on the sideboard by the tele-phone. He had a revolver tucked into his waistband. He seemed quite nice and said 'Good morning' in Polish. There were two more men in the living room. They were going through the drawers of the bureau, the family photographs and the luggage ready to be sent to Alexandria to the boat. Mother seemed cross but then it dawned on me that she was not in a bad temper; she was terrified, on the verge of hysteria. She was trying to tell one of the men that my father had left without his reading glasses. The two men bundled all the family snapshots and films into a paper bag and left. Right on the bureau lay a quilted sack which was full of gold coins. It looked like a sponge bag and they had not even looked inside.

We waited for my father to come back for two days and two whole nights. At one time during that first day we saw his car being driven away. It was a sign that everything was all right – he was going to come back soon in the car. My mother worried further, even about this – he could not drive back without his glasses. The following two nights were very long. My little sisters went to bed at the usual time while Mother and I sat in armchairs, dozing now and then. During the day my sisters and I played halfheartedly in the garden. As we were arguing who was going to be jungle girl and whose turn it was to be Tarzan, a woman called out to me. She was vaguely familiar. She asked me to go back inside to see my mother while she took little Biba upstairs to a neighbour's flat. I can't remember what happened to Beatrice. The living room door was shut. Doors were never shut at home except at Christmas when the tree was being decorated. When I opened the door I walked into a room full of people, strangers and half strangers. My mother was slumped in a chair and a man came forward and gently told me. I went to my mother; she hugged me and I couldn't cry. She told me she knew he was dead the night before. There had been a bird singing – birds don't usually sing in the night. She said he had spoken to her through the bird and told her not to worry.

The first day is never the worst because you can somehow slip back to the day before when there was still hope. Then there are calm intervals alternating with moments of dreadful recognition, more painful each time, and then slowly the reality takes over and there is just a permanent hurt.

Beatrice and I took it in turns to be with my mother, with the only relief coming from playing with Biba, the golden-haired happy six-year-old. My mother couldn't look at her without collapsing into tears. Early next morning there were a lot of birds singing. We never openly talked about my father again.

It was terrible to watch my mother trying to write letters to Father's sisters in Poland. It took her a whole day of starting, stopping and screwing up sheets of paper. My grandmother was very old and ill, so my father's death was kept secret from her for years. She couldn't understand why there were no letters from him, but the post was bad from Palestine, so lies could be told.

My father's family was so close that he and his two sisters were insep-arable. Grandma was a loving tyrant and Grandpa, who was like an angel to me, was of an old Polish family from Kiev. They had been landowners in the Ukraine, where my father was born in 1891, and his sisters within the next seven years. In one of the many wars between Poland and the Ukraine Grandpa lost his estates. He was already a qualified engineer and became very successful in that pro-fession. Grandpa designed the first electrical power plants to be built in Russia. He was also an exceptional entrepreneur and became one of the founders of Orbis, the Thomas Cook's of Poland at the time. His enterprise and talents quickly offset the loss of the family lands and the family continued to live the lives of Polish gentry.

The children, two sisters and Witold, were very talented. The elder sister, Zofia Hulanicka, became a famous pianist. She had been the only student of Paderewski. Halina was a prima ballerina with the leading Polish company, and shocked the family by dancing topless.

The family and friends played tennis, canoed and kayaked through the rivers of Poland in the summer and climbed in the Carpathians every spring. Winter was spent in Zakopane skiing and ice-skating. My father's talents were for gymnastics and diving. He was captain of the Polish Olympic team at the 1932 Olympics in Los Angeles. He travelled widely and wrote six mammoth books about his travels, which were never published. In World War I his family thought he had been killed. Two years after his 'funeral service' he walked through the front door and into his startled mother's arms. He had walked back to Poland, all the way from Russia.

In my mother's version of events he wooed and won the hearts of most of the beautiful women in Poland. Even after his second marriage, to my mother, the 'come up and see me some time' letters from former girlfriends never seemed to cease. His first marriage, to a society beauty, was childless. Clotilde was fragile, always unwell, and lay in bed surrounded by the latest medicines. She was a distinguished plastic surgeon, however, and became Sir Archibald McIndoe's assistant during World War II, rebuilding the faces of injured servicemen.

In 1928, through the influence of Zofia's first husband, who was the Governor of Warsaw, my father was posted to London as consul general. Life then was full of elegant parties and revelry, and regular travels between London and Warsaw. One Sunday in 1931, aged forty, he met my mother at a coffee party in London after church. He was smitten by her. It was love at first sight. This was his side of the story.

My mother's version was less glamorous. She was Polish, nineteen, and on holiday from finishing school in Eastbourne. The man, old enough to be her father, never left her side. Wherever she was taken socially by her chaperone he was there. At every Polish gathering he was there. As time went on his buoyant, arrogant manner slowly changed to that of a very lovesick man. In the carefree days of the early 1930s, Polish society in England moved around in groups to weekend parties, the races, and on motorcycle trips to Scotland. The pressures on my father who was still married, were considerable. It seems too civilized for words, but Clotilde's reaction was that he had to marry this girl if she would have him. With Clotilde's blessing the courtship was on. My father longed for a son, and Clotilde knew that she could not bear him children. Eventually their marriage was annulled. All this time my mother seemed to have little say in events. She was just overwhelmed by his love for her.

Mother had a very turbulent life. To this day I find it hard to understand, and there are many gaps I cannot fill. In those days people's way of life was so different. Mother's childhood was spent in convent schools, and she didn't seem to go home for holidays, yet she never felt anything but deepest love for her mother. She bore no resentment about her childhood except for remembering a few instances at the convent when she was left to kneel on dried peas for endless hours because she had committed some minor offence.

One day her father disappeared and left her and her brother alone with their mother. When she was eight, her father came back.

He didn't return alone. He was with a beautiful woman and a young girl who he said was his daughter, my Aunt Sophie. Grandfather disappeared again but my grandmother took both strangers in and looked after them. That Grandpa was never heard of again, at least not to my knowledge. The two girls were brought up together as sisters. My mother always claimed that Sophie was twelve years older than her, but Sophie's story was that the age difference was only eight years. My mother's version was that Sophie was born out of wedlock, yet years later my aunt told me behind the closed bathroom door in one of our 'little talks' that 'of course' Mother was the illegitimate one. This mystery seemed to be at the root of their love/hate relationship and the tension was passed on to me and my sisters. There was nothing but blood and thunder when Mother and Auntie were together in later years.

My aunt spent her life fabricating or embroidering stories and events. Some of them my mother would verify. At other times Auntie would relate pure fantasy, usually in front of Mother, with a challenging look in her eyes. Mother would keep silent for the sake of peace and quiet.

When my aunt was in her twenties she went to study music in America. There she met her future husband, whose family were prosperous proprietors of a newspaper in Poland. It was a match of convenience: at last my aunt had security, position, money and freedom. But it was a disaster: her husband turned out to be a real wastrel, a stage door Johnny who rapidly spent his fortune on showgirls and high living. After two years my aunt decided to divorce him. In those days divorce was social suicide and my aunt suffered a nervous breakdown, ending up in hospital with complete amnesia.

Auntie soon recovered from the shock of her divorce, however. Nothing could or would beat Auntie. She was a very lovely blonde, with deep-set steel blue eyes, rather a long nose, and not an ounce of excess flesh on her. She had delicate size 3 feet. These feet were to give me a complex for life, since I was blessed with size 7. She once told me how I must never attract attention to them because no man could ever fall in love with a woman who had such an abnormality.

Apart from being a beauty she had become fast thinking, strong as iron and very unemotional. This must have been rare in those days when women were bred to be limp, decorative and dependent on men. She must have been so emotionally bruised when she was young that she spun a cocoon around herself so as not to let any feeling out or admit weakness or failure. She always won at everything. If she could not win the games of others, she would make up her own and come first to the finishing line. My aunt wanted palaces and she got them, much later, through her second marriage to a very rich industrialist. Today she would have achieved them for herself without loveless relationships, and been very much happier.

While growing up, my mother was ferried between Grandma, her friends, and the convent with those dried peas. Still, she learned to embroider and sew as only nuns can teach. She loved to sew right to the end of her life, even when her eyes troubled her. She learned to scrub, clean and launder. She was shuttled between Grandma's friends on her holidays. One holiday my aunt discovered that she was staying in Paris with a woman who was said to be a courtesan. Auntie hurriedly collected her and thus started many years of a curious and sporadic guardianship.

This was in 1930. Auntie was now free but divorced – a scarlet woman with a small sister as a kind of chaperone. She had good jewellery but little money. An ordinary woman in those days and in those circumstances would have been paralysed, but not Auntie. She sold her jewellery, first having perfect copies made of each piece. In the thirties every respectable woman had to sport impressive jewellery. Her next move, on the proceeds of her sales, was to rent a sumptuous apartment in the Avenue Victor Hugo in Paris, fully furnished with antiques. In her fabrications, the furniture came from family estates and my mother's recently employed governess was an old family retainer. My mother was trotted out every day at 4 o'clock in front of the gentlemen callers to recite poetry, wearing her sailor suit and with a gigantic organdie bow in her hair. After the recital she was whisked back to the kitchen to the company of friendly maids.

One afternoon in particular stayed in my mother's memory. The drawing room was empty when she entered. Disconcerted by the change of routine she was wondering if she should return to the kitchen or recite to the empty room when my aunt entered. She was alone and appeared to be nervous. She listened to the recital and then pointed to a large mirror with an ornate gold frame in a corner of the room. Left to herself, my mother would probably never have noticed that it was shattered, but my aunt firmly told her that she must not worry about it and sent her away. When she returned to the kitchen it was buzzing with rumours of gunshots and an angry lover, but the mirror was never referred to again and Mother was too frightened to ask.

There were trips to Deauville, the sisters exquisitely dressed, with an accompanying maid, and usually driven by a gentleman friend in a very fine automobile. There was more reciting, and tears if the verses were not memorized. One day it became too much, and Mother ran away. She was found by the police at a railway station, cold and hungry. She was never allowed to forget how ungrateful and selfish she was. Even we were reminded of her sin that day, thirty years later.

Then came a period of peace. My aunt fell in love with a Polish prince, impoverished as princes go, though not poor by today's standards. But a divorcee like Auntie was not suitable for him and he, with no money, was no match for her. Soon afterwards he made a correct marriage with a rich and aristocratic Polish beauty. Years later when news came that he had been killed in a car crash, my aunt was really upset, as I had never seen her before, with a grief she did not attempt to hide.

There was one particular admirer who seemed devoted to Aunt Sophie, and she exploited him shamelessly. Andrew Gassner had been patient for years, waiting for the right moment to ask her to marry him. My mother adored him. Life was almost normal when he was around and my aunt became more relaxed and laughing. He nearly fulfilled her requirements – he was rich and of noble background – but he was fat! Eventually my aunt agreed to marry him. The honeymoon was spent on a train to India. Mother, who was sixteen, went along as far as Belgrade. The bridal couple had separate compartments with a 'Do Not Disturb' sign always on Auntie's door. Andrew was not allowed into her compartment before 10 o'clock in the morning and then usually only in my mother's presence. My mother and Andrew played cards throughout this part of the honeymoon, commiserating with each other about Auntie's behaviour.

After this my mother was sent to a finishing school in Eastbourne. My aunt planned that my mother should marry a cousin of Andrew's, thus securing the Austrian share of the fortune. So when Auntie returned from one of her voyages to find my mother practically at the altar with a divorced man of forty, her anger probably made my mother even more determined to marry my father. She was cut out of the Gassner inheritance – for the first of many times.

It seems rather romantic now that my mother and father were actually forced to elope. The child bride was brought home to Poland. Grandmother couldn't believe her eyes that this young girl of twenty was the cause of all the scandal and shame of a divorce. She was very lovely, with terrified huge brown eyes, tall, skinny and gawky. Her silk stockings were hanging in folds round her ankles – her clothes were still part of a school uniform. My mother had never been allowed to voice any opinion or make a decision, and now she was terrified. Zofia and Halina, my father's sisters, were strong and welcoming. For anyone whom Witold loved so much, their hearts and doors were wide open. After the wedding ceremony there followed a time of security and happiness. Even Grandma thawed. The gawky child turned into a swan. The wrinkled stockings revealed magnificent long legs. How sad none of us inherited those legs!

I was born in December 1936. Although my father desperately wanted a male heir, he was overjoyed. He insisted the next baby would certainly be a boy. Meantime I took the centre of the stage. Grandpa was out of his mind with happiness. I had his square jaw and square head – I was Grandpa's girl. Grandma, too, was delighted. Witold had been the end of the line, but now there was a continuation of the family tree.

In 1938 Father was appointed Polish consul general in the Middle East. With us came our Polish nanny, Olga, and two White Russian maids. A household was set up in the Polish consulate, an enormous Arab house on the edge of Jerusalem, surrounded by fields and tended by numerous servants, including Jacob, a Palestinian Bedouin boy that Father rescued from poverty, who was houseboy and remained with us for years. When he was a grown man he brought his bride to show to my father. He had paid a hundred pounds for her, a high price, as she was educated and bilingual.

We quickly settled into our new life, and soon after our arrival my sister Beatrice was born. By now Auntie had forgiven Mother for marrying my father and sailed down the Mediterranean with Andrew in their huge motor yacht for my christening in Bethlehem. I was two, rather old for this ceremony, but my parents had wanted to wait until they could christen me on the actual spot where Jesus was born. After the christening my mother and father went on a cruise on the yacht with Auntie. They got as far as Beirut! Father could only take that much of Auntie. Auntie could not accept defeat and swamped Mother with parcels of clothes from Paris: cartwheel hats, gloves and shoes, baby clothes by the ton. But there was always an admonishing letter in the parcel that turned everything sour.

The time came to go home on leave to Poland. We reached Warsaw in 1939 and went to the country to visit Grandma and Grandpa. It was a very hot summer. I romped with Martynka and Crystopher, my cousins, in the giant playpen on the river bank. My elder cousin, Marek, was there as well. The next time I was to speak to him was forty-three years later.

While we were there, Father went to the Foreign Office. Orders came that we were to pack and immediately set off for Gdansk to board the SS *Batory*, a liner leaving for the Middle East. After tearful goodbyes and a sudden departure we reached the boat. There was chaos. Jewish refugees were crushed on the decks, and sleeping in gangways. It was a long, painful journey.

Hitler invaded Poland three days after we sailed. We were safe but all our relatives were to experience hell. The husbands of both my Polish aunts were thrown into concentration camps. Fragments of news would reach us at intervals. One uncle died, the other lived for a short period after being set free at the end of the War. My Aunt Halina was caught by the Germans and was for many years in Auschwitz. Grandpa died of cancer but Grandma only gave up when she heard her son was dead.

In 1982, I discovered three cousins still alive: Marek, architect and dean of a university in the USA, and Martynka and Crystopher, living in Poland.

Chapter Two

By the age of six I was already quite fastidious and determined about my likes and dislikes in clothes. My mother dressed Beatrice and me like identical dolls. If I disliked the short red gingham dresses with matching knickers, the little red bows in our hair, white socks and scarlet pumps, I disliked much more the 'aah's' and 'ooh's' and 'aren't they lovely' that went with wearing these outfits. I wanted to be different from my sister, who was eighteen months younger. My mother agreed to dress me in the same style but a different colour. She had sailor dresses made for us from parachute silk, given to my father by a soldier. To this day I dislike any form of sailor clothes.

For skiing holidays in Lebanon we had white woolly sheepskin coats with hoods made for us. I had to be different so mine had no hood. In the summer we would go to Beirut. It was full of French influence and the shoe shops in particular were spectacular. Mother was dotty about bright platform peeptoe slingback sandals, and my father would buy her dozens of pairs to take back to Jerusalem. On those holidays we children couldn't wait to get back to the beach and eat Arab ice cream, which was like chewing gum.

My mother always looked beautiful. She had lovely clothes, spectacular hats, and white gloves on Sundays. When I started to go to school in Jerusalem with children whose parents had suffered in the War, I began to feel guiltily self-conscious about her looks. My friends' parents were so grey and tired and unhappy that in contrast Mother looked as if she was in Technicolor. After a tea party at home I would secretly give away my clothes and toys to my friends. My mother would then stand at the door and collect all the articles, which sometimes included her dresses, as the children left. I felt I could be equal with them if I did not have all those possessions. Mother didn't scold me. She just said I was too like my father. He would have given everything away if she hadn't stopped him.

In every classroom of our Polish school there was a photograph of King George VI and Queen Elizabeth. All the photographs were masked to show only their heads, as the teachers considered that Her Majesty's dress revealed an indecent amount of cleavage.

Beatrice and I used to beg Mother to draw pretty faces for us. We would sit watching mesmerized as she drew the most beautiful little heads. I remember getting quite angry with her when she grew tired and the faces started to look less pretty.

As children, Beatrice and I spent our time on the beach swimming and playing. Beatrice was a beautiful baby, a little knot of energy. Her hair was white and her eyes were like black coals. Her energy attracted everyone's attention. As long as it wasn't my father's, I didn't mind. The moment his eyes remained longer than a second on her I felt pangs of jealousy. Mother always said I was of his blood and Beatrice of hers. My mother's attention to her only occasionally bothered me. I had eyes only for my father. I never wanted a child of mine to feel this jealousy and that is why Witold, my own son, is an only child.

When my sister Biruta, abbreviated to Biba, was born I did not feel the rejection I had felt when Beatrice stole my limelight. Biba was six years younger and she was like a little live dolly. She was a most beautiful baby and, although she had been another try for a male heir, my father adored her. She grew prettier and prettier each day. Beatrice and I were now in competition for attention. Biba, too, was christened in Bethlehem.

When I was eight I was ready for my first communion. I had by then decided to be a saint. I had visited every local shrine and I prayed morning and evening. Everywhere we went had some holy significance. I had touched the spot where Jesus was born, where he walked, where he was laid when he was dead, and now I was to have my holy communion where Jesus had his last supper. I wasn't the only one who was going to be a saint – all my friends were going to join me, too.

The night before our first communion we were all staying in the Polish house (Dom Polski) in Jerusalem. After confessing our mortal sins we were not allowed to eat or drink until the following morning. My mother found me, lying on the floor, looking a bit blue. I thought it would be a sin to swallow my saliva. My mother and father took hours to explain to me that God did not want to see me dead before I had taken my first holy communion. I could become a saint later on in life.

*

My mother sent food and clothing parcels to friends in Warsaw. So-called friends of my father came to Jerusalem to get him to return to Poland with them. The communists couldn't afford to have too many patriots outside their control, free to tell the world what was really happening in Poland. When he couldn't be persuaded to return they would start the propaganda on us children, telling us stories of our grandmother waiting to see us, of our aunts and cousins, until we would pester our father to go back to Poland. I remember him turning to my mother and saying, 'Now they've got at the children.' When VE Day was announced on the radio, my father wept. He said it was the end of Poland. He joined the merrymaking at the officers' club in Jaffa that night but with a heavy heart. He would never go back to a communist Poland. On no account would we ever stop speaking Polish. We would be leaving Palestine one day, maybe for Brazil, where many Poles had emigrated. At night he would listen to the radio in the dark. Some programmes came from the BBC in London, broadcast by his friend Joe Zaranski, now married to Clotilde. Other nights we sat with no lights on listening to a piano recital by Zofia, my aunt, in Poland. She played Chopin sonatas which made my father weep, and we in turn wept for him. He was suffering so much and there was nothing we could do to help him.

My father had many friends, Poles, Jews and Arabs. At Christmas our house looked like an off-licence, littered with crates of wine, whisky and brandy. As my father never smoked or drank, Mother's kitchen cupboards were bulging with liquor. Friends who had escaped from Poland arrived one day with a suitcase of Polish money, their only possession. They gave us children the banknotes to play with. The zlotys were worth nothing, but we loved to use them for our games.

Every time a letter arrived from Auntie, Mother would be thrown into the depths of depression. My father would comfort her, saying she was safe from Auntie now, but the many years of her sister's oppression had carved a deep scar. I learned to loathe this aunt of mine who made my mummy cry so much. My parents were usually so happy and jolly together. They had fights, and sometimes my mother would throw a few plates at my father, but they always ended up laughing and cuddling and saying sorry.

As consul general for the Middle East, my father had a very complicated task. The Polish government had sent a delegation to

London in 1936, headed by Prime Minister Beck. Many Polish Jews were Zionists and wanted to emigrate to Palestine. The Poles thrashed out a deal whereby the British would accept an unlimited number of Zionists, provided their wealth was moved in merchandise and not in money. This obviously suited Poland, whose economy would have been undermined by a mass exit of Jewish capital. Poland decided to subsidize the less affluent Jews who wished to leave, and it was part of my father's work to supervise the welfare of these poorer immigrants when they arrived in Palestine. Inevitably this brought him into close contact with the extremist Jewish organizations, principally with the extreme revisionist party, the Irgun, and its terrorist offshoot, the Stern Gang. This party was the predecessor of today's Heruth party, headed by Menachem Begin, who in the early 1940s was in Palestine and was rumoured to have deserted from the Polish army.

In 1939 the Polish government was taken over by General Sikorski, a vindictive man who promptly started settling old scores. He dismissed a large number of diplomats who he felt had been so loyal to the old regime that they would not give him full support. My father, who was a great admirer of Josef Pilsudski, a former Prime Minister, received a telegram in September 1939 telling him that he had been replaced, thanking him for his efforts and giving him until 16 December that year to resign.

England, at war, was desperate to keep the friendship of the Arab nations who had seen the attempts to partition Palestine as the thin end of the wedge to its total annexation by the Zionists. My father, who had friends in and contacts with the Arab world as well as with the Zionists, was welcomed by the British with open arms. He was made chief censor for the Middle East.

He was only too pleased to leave the ornate French furniture of the consulate, but we took our own precious treasures. Father packed his collection of Persian carpets and sabres that had been presented to him by his Arab friends. Mother didn't appreciate his collection of Arab art. He had made himself a den filled with Persian carpets, ceremonial sabres encrusted with jewels, and mother-of-pearl inlaid furniture. He would sit there on cushions smoking a *nargila*. Our baby hands and feet had been pressed into clay tiles decorated with Arabic writing and mounted on the wall. We had no furniture, but many Islamic treasures.

We moved to Tel Aviv and lived for a while in a modern block of flats. Many soldiers from the Polish Army visited us before going on to Tobruk. They left their watches and trinkets in my mother's care in case they were killed. None of them returned from the battle. The bomb raids were now quite frequent. The Italian Air Force dropped their leftover bombs on Tel Aviv and Haifa on the way back from desert raids. We spent many nights in the bomb shelter of the apartment block. My father couldn't stand the claustrophobic feeling or the wails as the bombs fell – he would go off for a walk in the deserted streets to watch the explosions. The sky was filled with red sparks. He enjoyed looking death between the eyes. On his return he would tell my panic-stricken mother there had been little danger.

Then we moved to a beautiful house in Sarona, near Tel Aviv, outside the barbed wire gates of the interned German colony. Our neighbours were British. My mother could not understand why they looked undernourished, as local food supplies were more than sufficient. She was shocked when her neighbour told her that they only ate what was the allowed ration in England – one egg a week, and hardly any meat. My mother thought they were mad but my father said it was most noble.

When father came home from work I would take our tea to the orchard at the bottom of the garden. Sometimes we would have it perched on the lower branches of a guava tree, slowly working our way through many ripe fruits. On other days we would make a change by climbing up the sturdier fig tree that grew a few yards away. Often Father would become too ambitious and climb so high for the fruit that we had trouble getting him down later. He would sit there silently perched on a branch and we would know he was just working out how he would get down. While we ate our exotic fruits, like a couple of monkeys, he would tell me how one day when we got to England we would eat fruit called strawberries with whipped cream, and go to the woods to look for tiny wild ones. Our teatime menu never included bananas, as the banana tree was seething with black spiders, sometimes with deadly tarantulas.

My father was also president of the Polish YMCA. He spent much of his free time helping the poor parentless cadets who had been separated from their families. Our school in Jerusalem had been full of children of Poles who had been through the Holocaust. They had been to Siberia, and had survived the Russian winter eating dogs and cats and even digging up dead animals that had been soaked in petrol to prevent them from being eaten. They had seen real horrors. I felt ashamed that my life had been so happy and so full of security and I felt left out. I wanted to be one of them. When my father drove us to school I would ask him to let us off a few blocks away so nobody would see we had a car.

Jerusalem had been divided into Arab and Jewish zones. Our apartment was in the Jewish zone, which was much more civilized to live in. There were modern comforts and supplies of butter, eggs and sugar. To get to school we walked through fields with olive trees, past the American YMCA opposite the famous King David Hotel. Beyond the fields we entered the British zone, where the school was. After the King David Hotel was blown up we couldn't go to school for many months as it was impossible to get there without risking a sniper's shot. We thought it was all marvellous fun but my mother lived in dread every evening waiting for my father to come home. At six in the evening there was a curfew and everyone had to be indoors. We used to sneak out and play in the fields beside the house.

Later my sister and I had to go away and join some other Polish children up in a boarding school run by nuns on a hill above the Arab town of Ain Karem. Early one Saturday morning, when we hadn't heard from my father for a couple of weeks, the Polish priest came up to the house on the hill. He said we were to get dressed quickly and come with him. He was going to take us to our father. When we had dressed he said we were not to take anything with us. This annoyed me but eight miles later, as we climbed over rocks and hills, avoiding the main road, I was quite pleased I wasn't carrying anything. We were baffled why we had to walk for such a long way. Sometimes we could see the main road. There were stone boulders across it. As we walked through the fields covered with spring flowers and poppies that were as thick as a carpet we sang Polish songs. Eventually, exhausted, we descended from the hill on to the main road. It was thick with cement blocks. There had been a battle. Behind a boulder was my father. He was weeping as we ran into his arms. We grumbled that we had had to leave school. The priest walked back to Ain Karem and we went home by car. There had been many battles between the Jewish town and Ain Karem. All communications there had been cut off. My mother and father were desperate to get us back, not knowing if we were still alive, but all I could think of was when I was going back to school again. After we came home some mornings we would go out and inspect the bullet holes in a friend's house higher up the road after a battle the previous night. It was all such fun for us children. We had heard the explosion when the King David Hotel was blown up. My mother and father looked so depressed afterwards: so many of their friends had been killed. When the whole main street in Jerusalem was blown up by terrorists our windows shattered all over the flat.

Through the more peaceful times we had spent marvellous holidays in camps for the Polish orphans near Jaffa surrounded by orange groves. We played on white sandy beaches collecting pumice stones. The sea was full of Portuguese men-of-war jellyfish, but we could swim and dive in the water reservoirs of the orange groves, which were like large concrete swimming pools. When we were blue with cold we had hot cocoa and lumps of chocolate to warm us up before flaking out on the camp beds in the army tents. When dusk fell we crept around washing and going to the loo with no lights on so as not to attract flying insects, centipedes and tarantulas. Every moment seemed to be a new adventure.

As I grew up my father kept his anguish from us all. He must have been tormented by what was happening to his country and his family. His work was dangerous but our home life was happy.

In 1943 Jerusalem was still like a frontier town. There were lots of cafés and shoe shops but the clothes shops were few and far between. Usually our clothes were made by a seamstress who came to the house; sometimes mother made them herself. We spent that whole year preparing our wardrobes for our new life in England where we planned to go but where we knew there was heavy clothes rationing. Mother decided to store up clothes for the future. We had red tartan dresses and lots of other outfits made in lovely bright colours. We would be set up for the next few years while the rationing continued. I made my mother comb every shop for shoes in the right shade of red. I didn't like the dark red colour that Beatrice had chosen. We stocked up on wool socks and underwear. Our home began to look like a warehouse. Mother's other worry was that we would starve in England as news had reached her of how small the rations were. She spent days melting butter and pouring the liquid into tins. There were jumbo jars of jams, flour, rice, spiky cones of sugar, tea, coffee and even Lux soap flakes. We had enough provisions to keep a battalion of soldiers fed for a year.

When the Polish school was closed down, my father bought every Polish teaching book in Palestine. They would have been censored or destroyed otherwise. I shall never forget my mother's unprintable words when a crate of a thousand books was delivered to our home. The problem was that as they were school books most of them were duplications of the same volume. She said my father was crazy – he *was* a little bit. Frequently he bought her a present of a blouse or dress or anything he thought she might like. If he couldn't decide which colour, he would bring all the colours available. Every week was like Christmas with him, full of surprises and excitement.

On one of his mysterious trips to Beirut he bought Mother a dozen of what must have been the first French bikinis. I shall always remember the horror on her face as she examined a huge box of woollen two-piece bathing suits. The woolly knickers went up to the waist and the top almost reached them in the middle. They were knitted in very thick yarn and decorated with multicoloured woolly balls. My mother was shocked by the scanty size and said she would never wear such a rude costume – but she did, and the first bulky megakini was tested in the crystal clear waters of Lake Tiberias. Mother wasn't even able to float. She sank very slowly as the bathing suit filled with water. Only her nose rested above the surface. Her bikini was waterlogged, and the straps of the top began to stretch. We all watched on the shores of the lake where Jesus once walked on water, convulsed in stitches as she pleaded for help. The other bikinis never got wet.

We would listen spellbound to my father's stories of how beautiful England was. The grass was so green. The trees were so different from the exotic evergreens and palms. Their leaves turned red and fell off in the winter and in the spring, as if touched by a fairy wand, everything turned to emerald green. One day he would take us on a train journey. We had never seen a real train. He would also take us on the underground. Our eyes would widen as he described the underground tunnels that ran underneath the city of London. But what excited us most were the tales of self-service cafeterias.

In Jerusalem our life was spent amongst Byzantine architecture and streets where Jesus had once walked. We travelled in horse-drawn buggies and the thought of getting on a double-decker scarlet bus was riveting. Every Sunday we would trek by foot with the Polish Girl Scouts to visit a holy monument, basilica or shrine. When there was no trip my father would take us to Jaffa to the officers' club or to the beach, or sometimes inland to the Dead Sea. I hated the Dead Sea. Like all children I was usually covered in cuts and bruises, and when I entered the sticky salt water the stinging became intolerable. You had to be careful not to splash because if a drop of water got into the eyes you were immediately blinded and it took some time to wash the salt water out. If you swallowed any water you vomited.

One weekend as we were setting out for a picnic my father went to the post box in the entrance of the flats. He drew out an envelope addressed to him. As he read it he became very still. My mother took it out of his hand and looked at it. She began crying and my father put his arm around her. That Sunday, as we chattered and played, my mother and father were very quiet. After my father was shot my mother told me it was the third anonymous letter he had received saying that he was going to be killed.

We were going to Alexandria to catch a banana boat to England. My father was to follow us in May. There was going to be trouble and he wanted us safely tucked away. All my Polish friends had left us to go to camps in Cyprus before being sent to England. I begged my father to let us go with them. He told me we were lucky not to have to live in camps as the others had to. All the trunks were lined up all over the flat. I watched my father carefully painting 'Not Wanted On Voyage' on each one.

The night before we were due to leave for England we had a surprise visitor. It was Heniek Herold, my father's godson. He was the son of my parents' closest friend from Hertzlyja. It was a strange visit, out of the blue. Heniek wanted to see the flat. He was very jumpy and nervous, and left soon afterwards. It was after he left that my father gave me his pen. He knew something was going to happen. We went to bed early, excited about our journey the following day. I wonder if my mother slept that night. I don't think my father did. I think he knew it was his last night.

Four years later my aunt took my mother, Beatrice and me to see the Festival of Britain on the South Bank in London. As we walked round the exhibition we passed a bench. A young man sat there frozen, looking at my mother. It was Heniek, my father's godson. If I had known he had been a party to my father's death, I would have killed him with my bare hands then and there.

After the War my father had left his job as chief censor for the Middle East and become director of the international YMCA. His connections with the Zionist organizations and amongst the Arabs meant that he was chosen as a mediator for the United Nations in the violent disputes over the partitioning of Palestine. Initially his efforts were supported by the Haganah, one of the Jewish groups who wanted to cooperate with both the British and the Arabs. To the extremists of the Irgun, now led by Menachem Begin, a mediator in my father's position, with the support of moderates on all sides, was a major threat to their plans for the total extinction of the Palestinian Arabs.

My father's name was at the top of the list of those to be exterminated. They took him blindfolded to a deserted house on the outskirts of Jerusalem to join another victim waiting to be killed. They were both shot through the temple, and a few days later they were found rotting in a heap by the Palestine police. Everything of value had disappeared, even the gold fillings of their teeth. My grandfather's signet ring was gone. It was a huge ornate ring that had been made of gold leaf scraped off the ceiling of Wavel Castle in Cracow in the Middle Ages, and passed from father to son for generations. I know I'm going to find that ring one day. It belongs to Witold, my son.

We buried my father's remains on the Mount of Olives and left for England the following week. Israelis have proudly told me I should go and see Jerusalem as it is now. The Mount of Olives is full of beautiful buildings – the graveyard for transit Poles is there no more. I just don't feel like seeing fancy buildings standing on my father's grave.

Mama said she had been too happy – it couldn't last. For the past fourteen years Mama had been lavished with love and protection. In Papa's eyes she could do no wrong. Nothing was good enough for her. He doted on her, protected her and spoiled her shamelessly. She in turn doted on her babies, substitutes for the dolls she never had. She spent all her time on her home and children, cuddled and

19

nourished them with unselfish love. My mother gave us all the security she had missed as a child. She could enter a barren room and make it into a home with her love and energy. She fed us nourishing foods until we were stuffed like little piglets. She was unprepared for the end of her good fortune. Her only escape was the thought that death would wipe us all out together. When my father was gone all she could talk about was joining him with us. I wanted to be with him, but I didn't want to die.

The day after my father had been found, Mother was advised to leave the flat. With only a few possessions, our trunks left in the flat waiting to be closed, we were driven to a Polish friend's house in the Arab quarter. We would stay there until the next aeroplane evacuating British families was to leave for England. My father's English friends had secured seats for us. They came to help my mother. We weren't even British subjects but they gave us priority. It was a way of showing loyalty to my father even after his death.

We waited for news of the date of the flight. Every move was secret. My mother's friends lived in an enormous echoing Arab house. There was no furniture on the beautiful flagstones, only beds and a few essentials. We slept in a vaulted room in one bed. It was February and quite cold. Only one other room was occupied by our friends. Their son Janek had rigged out the house with booby traps near the windows in case of intruders. There were empty square tins filled with electric bulbs. Somehow he had arranged that if anyone tried to enter any of the windows, a piece of string would explode the light bulbs inside the tin and give a warning.

One evening an Arab came to the house and asked to use the phone. I was curled up in the corner watching him. He was not an Arab – he spoke Yiddish on the telephone. I knew a little Yiddish from playing with children in the neighbouring flats. The man was describing the inside of the house on the telephone. He thanked everyone very much and left. I told my mother what he had been saying. The next day we moved out to the American YMCA which faced the King David Hotel. I spent the next few days, in between fits of weeping, sending everyone crazy by riding up and down the lift of the tall tower.

One morning my mother said we were going to England. We put on our double-breasted coats, thick tights, and Winnie-the-Pooh felt hats, and set out on the journey to our new foreign life. My mother's fur coat was weighed down by gold coins sewn into the hem. We drove in a convoy of coaches and armoured trucks to Lydda airport, the armed soldiers in the trucks on the lookout for an ambush. We were too emotionally spent to be frightened. If we were to arrive safely it was God's will.

Chapter Three

Our young eyes were used to strong, bright light, sparkly tall white skyscrapers, white sands and clear blue skies. We landed at Croydon Airport in February 1948. My excitement was mounting. I couldn't wait to go to a Lyons self-service café, to travel on the underground and go for a ride on a double-decker bus. Someone called a taxi. It was a dark, smoggy day, and there were rows and rows of little grey houses. They seemed to go on for ever, miles and miles of them. Everything was barren, cold and grey. There weren't any people about.

The taxi took us to Brixton. The friends of my father's who had offered to look after us, a general and his wife, were there to meet us at the front door. The house was part of a strange, curvy, rust-coloured brick crescent. Inside the house was very grim. It looked unlived in. There were no flowers anywhere, whereas we always had so many at home. For lunch there was just a lump of yellow cheese and a tiny little dab of butter and thin, funny looking bits of square white bread. I was starving. The general and his wife served themselves first. I couldn't believe the portions – that's what our dolls were served on their tea plates. After lunch my mother unpacked. We just sat there stunned and still hungry, wondering what was going to happen next.

It wasn't very long before my aunt found us. She traced us on the Polish grapevine. There was a telephone call and Mother said Auntie was coming. I couldn't wait to meet this wicked Auntie. I wasn't sure if I was scared or excited, but something was going to happen.

I shall never forget the first time I saw her. She didn't look like a wicked witch. She was beautiful. She came through the door like a breath of fresh air. She smelled of flowers. I had never seen such a beautiful little hat – it was ice blue, covered with black net. The hat matched her crystal hard eyes. Her small hands were covered with rings and she was sparkling all over with diamonds. Her earrings – and this really baffled me – comprised one enormous black and one white pearl. Poor Auntie, I thought, one day I will buy you another white pearl so that you have a matching pair. But Auntie wasn't so poor – Andrew Gassner had died in 1943, leaving her his fortune. Outside the house a chauffeur was waiting in a large car.

Auntie said she would like to speak to my mother alone and we were sent out of the room. A little later I was called in and introduced to her. I liked her. She said she had heard about my father on the radio and moved heaven and earth to find us. She ran her fingers across the dresser. They left a great shiny stripe – the furniture was really dusty. We were paying guests in this house, and she asked my mother how much she was charged. On hearing the sum she roared with laughter and said we might as well move into the Ritz with her for that. She had been living at the Ritz since Andrew Gassner's death. We packed again and said goodbye to the general and his wife.

The Ritz looked like a museum to me. Everyone seemed to walk around speaking in hushed voices. The central reception room was lovely, with that nice sound of running water from the fountain, and a rude plaster lady with no clothes on. I tried not to look. The teas were quite something. There were dainty sandwiches with all that crunchy grass on them, and cakes my aunt said were called 'a thousand leaves'. But this luxury could not go on for ever. Mother moved us into service apartments in Chesham Place near Belgrave Square.

At first life seemed comfortable and aimless. There were new customs to get acquainted with and new sounds to the ear. Auntie had ordered that Polish was not to be spoken any more. We were now in a new country and there was no point in holding on to a useless language. I had many sleepless nights worrying what my father would have said. On no account, he had told my mother, were we to forget the language, and if there was no Polish school we should have tuition after school to keep up with a Polish curriculum. I felt I was committing a mortal sin – not that we would keep up for more than a few hours in our new language. I had always thought that my English was rather good at school, but now it was hell. I was forever being corrected in pronunciation and grammar.

A Miss Smith was hired as governess and child-minder. I call her Miss Smith because she never made any impression on me. I cannot remember her real name or her face or her character. I didn't like her or dislike her. She was a phantom. Miss Smith was instructed to show us London and teach us English at the same time. We trotted from one museum to the next, Big Ben, the Zoo, Westminster Abbey, and, most tedious of all, the Schoolboys' Exhibition. I thought I would die with boredom watching all those trains on tracks. At meal-times we played 'I spy with my little eye'. We never went to the cafeterias where you could put coins in the slot, or on the under-ground trains. It wasn't the adventure my father had promised me. After our walk around London we would go to the Ritz for tea with Auntie. Miss Smith would report to her on our day. Then it was our turn to describe in broken English what we had done, being prompted and corrected as we went along.

At first I was quite happy to open up and try, but as time went on the meetings with Auntie became more and more frightening. There was never a pat on the back. My English seemed to get worse, not better; and I was becoming frightened of opening my mouth. It must have been extremely funny for Miss Smith to hear this very foreign lady with a very thick accent attempt to teach dumbstruck children how to pronounce English words. But Auntie never had much patience with children so Miss Smith would soon be sent packing with us back to the apartment and Mother's arms. Evenings were fun, full of laughter, Polish babble and lots of kisses and cuddles.

At this time started the dreaded ritual of the Sunday lunch which was to continue for the next eight years. Nothing, but nothing, would break the routine of those agonizing hours. At first there was a man who made things quite fun. His name was Ralph. He had been King George VI's private secretary. We usually saw him at those Sunday lunches. He was madly in love with Auntie and she was jolly and viv-acious when he was around, and he used to tick her off about nagging us so much. But their relationship didn't last.

One day came an order from my aunt. We were all to move to Brighton, to the seaside where the air was better for children. Beatrice and I were each given a holdall for our books and small per-sonal belongings. I shall never forget the excitement of that bag. I packed and unpacked it daily – we were going on a train journey at last. I had still never been on a train. We travelled on the Brighton Belle, and sat at little tables. Each one had a lovely brass lamp with a pink petal-edged lampshade. At my feet was my precious holdall, filled with books, exercise books, drawings and pencils.

At Brighton Station we parted company. Mother and we three

children went to stay at the Clarges Hotel at the Brighton Rock end of the seafront and Auntie took up residence in a suite on the first floor of a gin palace, the Metropole Hotel. The next-door suite was occupied then by Ralph.

My aunt claimed that her new home had always been Mr Churchill's favourite suite in Brighton, but now Auntie took possession. Mr Churchill never visited the Metropole again and was forced to change to the Royal Albion. Auntie was soon running the first floor of the hotel and particularly the pantry. The hotel staff were under her thumb. During the quiet of the week my aunt roamed round the other suites and removed any furniture she felt was appropriate for her apartments. There were ornate French glass cabinets, marble sideboards, tables and chairs. The sofas were re-covered in oyster damask, carpets were changed to soft mushroom, and the elegant plaster panelled walls were carefully painted in bleached magnolia. Her heavy drapes over giant windows were half drawn until midday to shelter her eyes from the blinding south light of the seafront.

Auntie's best-trained and most subservient waiter, Ernest, a wiry Austrian exile, liked a little gin now and then when she was out of the room. His habit was soon detected and a singing crystal decanter was installed. Just a slight vibration or at most a movement would start it chiming out 'It's a long way to Tipperary'. Poor Ernest must have been paralysed as he lifted that decanter for the first and last time. He was lectured and forgiven.

Adjoining the drawing room was the boudoir, whose door was never closed. Mirrored furniture was strategically placed at each corner of the room so that at any point my aunt could see what anybody was doing in the drawing room or who might be entering stealthily with a pass key.

I was always amazed by my aunt's boundless energy. It took me many years to realize that if you wake at midmorning you can actually function until the early hours of the following day. Her life was led like clockwork. The preparation for the coming day was a spectacular performance. Her personal maid, who was responsible for the wardrobe and belongings, would arrive at 10 o'clock. She would take in the morning tray of coffee and melba toast and the *Financial Times*, so that Auntie could check her investments. (*The Times* and *Telegraph* were flicked through at a quarter to one, before luncheon.) After a birdlike breakfast, my aunt spent an hour in the bathroom, another hour on her make-up, wearing a flowing peach satin peignoir, and the next hour on her coiffure.

As a youngster I was sometimes allowed to watch this ritual. My aunt had beautiful fine blonde hair. It was permed and reached below her shoulders. It was brushed vigorously and then out came this monstrous silver gadget called a glove stretcher, which was a forerunner of electric curling tongs. Her lovely fluffy hair was then side-parted and layers of fat sausages at asymmetrical levels were rolled and invisibly pinned. One big one was positioned at the top of the right temple and the next at a lower level on the other side, and so on to the nape of the neck. The finished result turned the hard little face even harder.

Then came the jewellery which in the mornings was sedate and discreet. At teatime Auntie changed into a little crêpe frock of pearl grey or sludge green, and the jewels became bolder. By the evening the tea gown made its appearance and we were ready for a state occasion in the jewel stakes. The tea gown was a long garment made of silk, velvet, crêpe or brocade, somewhere between an evening dress and a dressing gown. This was the finale of the informal routine. The formal version took at least two days to perfect.

At the formal evenings, which were quite frequent during this period, Mother sometimes attended. Auntie usually lent her some intricate gown. We children were, of course, not included. Auntie's friends were visitors from London, usually wealthy society people and MPs. These evening soirées ended with a game of chemmy, over which my aunt reigned, usually scooping up the winnings. She would have run a casino if gambling had been legal. Her guests were carefully chosen for their gaming abilities. At times they stayed the weekend in adjoining suites or the neighbouring Grand Hotel. Slowly her social circle grew in Brighton. The passport to Auntie's friendship was usually wealth or position, and preferably noble birth as well.

Most of my aunt's elaborate wardrobe was smuggled in from Paris by wealthy women who were short of cash. Their well-heeled husbands spent fortunes on sables and jewels but the poor ladies never seemed to have a cab fare in their crocodile handbags, so they resorted to running couture wardrobes to more financially independent widows. As stunning as my aunt looked in her fineries, it was her stockings that attracted unfavourable attention among her gossipy friends. She was passionately attached to peach-coloured, thick lisle hosiery. These unaccountably appeared with crêpe de Chine ensembles, satins and sables. My mother's one precious pair of glass nylons (as the earliest sheer stockings were known), extracted by my father in Jerusalem from a visiting American serviceman, were taboo. They were only worn by 'cheap women'. I was given that pair of glass nylons when they were beyond repair. They were my greatest treasure and I longed for the day when I would be old enough to wear them.

Auntie felt our hotel was an unsuitable place for young children, so she found us a large flat in a converted Victorian mansion facing Preston Park. The furniture, Persian carpets and all our possessions had at last arrived on the banana boat. Mother could have a lovely, light, pretty home again. But Auntie took charge. What might have been a happy, bright home was turned into a drab, dank, sensible prison. The walls were painted grey so they wouldn't show children's fingermarks, the curtains in the living room were of dark brown canvas with a revolting ochre braid. The sofa was brown so that it would wear well. It looked like a waiting room in Harley Street. My mother was allowed to have sunny yellow satin cotton curtains in her bedroom – but the remaining furnishings were of my aunt's choice. She even sent round a white marble bust of herself sculptured in the 1930s. This was placed on a cabinet by the telephone. I was going to please Auntie and paint her eyes and lips with my watercolours. The face of the bust needed some pupils and a little pink on the cheeks. It must have been my guardian angel who stopped me touching up the marble. I don't think that even my watercolour paint would have come off that porous stone. Mother seemed to accept all her commands quietly even though Auntie was not paying, but at night, when my aunt left the flat after seeing to carpenters, carpet layers and other workmen, my mother would turn into a raving tigress. Her coffers were emptying fast and her hopes of any independence diminished with each bill.

Our English was slowly improving and we could go to school. I was so excited; I could pack my little holdall again. Beatrice and I were to go to the local convent only a mile away. We were to be boarders. Why I cannot now imagine, but I loved the idea of boarding school.

I shall never forget my first night. I couldn't understand anything the welcoming nun said to me. All night I couldn't sleep with worrying about the next day, and Beatrice had a hacking cough. The nun kept coming in and angrily telling her to stop coughing, or so I imagined. The following days were even worse. The classes were enormous, at least thirty or forty girls. I couldn't understand anything the teacher said. I sat there mortified. I was made to read aloud. It sounded all right to me but I couldn't understand a word of what I had read. I sat there all term not knowing what anybody was talking about.

At the end of the term came 'retreat'. We walked the grounds for three days in silence and meditation. After retreat there was to be confession. For three days and nights I lived through hell. How could I say confession in English? I didn't even know how to say the opening words, 'Bless me Father, for I have sinned.' The moment came when I was in the queue for the confessional. There were hundreds of us. The priest was talking far too loudly in the box and it seemed everyone could hear what was being said. I was quaking with fear and embarrassment. But now it was my turn to go into the confessional. There was a wall of girls crowding behind me. I was in the box and there was silence. I was crying. The priest said so softly, 'What's the matter, child?' I must have said something that made him realize what my problem was. He helped me confess my lies, my rudeness to my aunt and all those other sins I couldn't remember.

After that day things seemed to become unblocked. I started to understand English. I still came thirty-ninth at the end of the term. My aunt gave me hell when she received the report, but it didn't matter too much. The worst was over.

The first lady of my dreams was Esther Williams. I loved her swimming when I'd seen the films in Palestine. Now I cut out every photograph I could find of her and pasted it in a pale blue scrapbook, and I practised her toothy, mindless smile. When we went swimming I was Esther Williams diving into the depths and coming out with eyes and mouth open with that plastic grin. I could do her fancy crawl without submerging the head. I swam and swam and swam. Mother said Esther was awful, her legs were too short – that was why she was photographed on tiptoes all the time – and her shoulders were like those of a Channel swimmer. I liked her even more for her imperfections. If one of her films was showing during the holidays I would go day after day to see it and sit right through all the performances from beginning to end.

In the local fleapit I became obsessed with films. I saw every film that came along, over and over. I devoured film magazines for hours and spent all my pocket money on them. I lived through the film stars. I had many other favourites, but nobody could touch Esther Williams. I practised the crawl on dry land. For certain, when I grew up I was going to be a swimming star. I hated her when she was out of water. In later films she seemed to be less and less often submerged. I sat with butterflies in my stomach ready for the water ballet. It was an awfully long wait – sitting half a day waiting for one sequence in each performance.

I would leave the cinema with my head in the clouds. I couldn't talk to anybody. My sisters were always making so much noise. I needed to be alone with my dreams. I liked my room – at least I didn't have to share it with anybody. My bed was lovely. It had a great dip in the mattress. I could really burrow into it, with the bedcovers over my head and only my cold nose poking out. My mother always had a cold nose in bed so I crocheted her a little nose cosy in fluffy yellow wool to keep the cold out. She couldn't use it, it made her sneeze. She seemed more of a sister than a mother – her problems seemed to be mine. My mother loved me very much but I'm not sure that she really liked me. I didn't have the knack of soothing her – I couldn't tell her untruths just to make her feel comfortable. Beatrice seemed to have a way to calm her. I always told Mother the truth of a situation, which was not always what she wanted to hear.

Mother was only thirty-six and life had apparently ended for her. She just hoped she would die soon as she couldn't go on living without my father. She was just marking time, washing and pressing for us to be immaculate. She darned the heels of our socks on a wooden mushroom. They began to look like intricate tapestries. They hurt a bit when they were in the shoes, but they were beautiful, full of lovely patterns and textures. We had many pretty dresses in our cupboard but we could never wear those on Sundays as Auntie thought red and other bright colours were vulgar. Mother's cupboard was bulging with lovely frocks which she never seemed to wear. Rows and rows of high-heeled shoes that my father had bought her stood sadly in tidy ranks. The only ones she wore were wedge crêpe-soled lace-ups. I loathed those shoes and I hated that bottle green felt beret with sludge beige woolly pompoms that seemed to be sitting on top of the hat that came out every Sunday. Auntie always wore dizzy hats and dainty Minnie Mouse shoes and Mother always looked as if she had arrived from a farm. Auntie, however, seemed quite happy with the way Mother looked.

Mother still kept up her old routine of applying mounds of cleansing cream to her face, splashing it with rose water and massaging it with night cream for several minutes. Then out came the pipe cleaners and the ends of her hair were rolled into little knots. My hair, then down to my waist, was daily plaited by my mother. The plaiting had to be at just the right tension. I was obsessed about my plaits not being too loose or too tight, and they had to be just the right one millimetre above the ear. Sometimes she would cross the two plaits and tie each end behind the opposite ear with a ribbon bow.

I sometimes suffered acute pain in a silly little bone below the ankle. It was said to be because I was growing too fast. When I was fourteen, my feet were size 7 and I was told that I would eventually grow in proportion to my feet. This would have made me a giant of over six feet. I dreaded it. Surprise, surprise, I stopped growing at five feet five and a half inches. I was very solid. Mother said I would settle down eventually and lose weight, but those secret sweeties and chocolates were such a comfort.

It is strange how I realized I had been stealing. There were always pennies and silver pieces lying in a saucer in the kitchen or on my mother's dressing table and I took the coppers and put them in my matchbox. But one day I took a silver two-shilling piece and the next day another silver coin. Soon after my mother found my matchbox with my little hoard. Because of this I was looked on with suspicion for a long time afterwards. My sisters never seemed to get into any scrapes. They were always so good; I was the one causing trouble.

In 1950 Brighton was becoming the Jerusalem of the British Isles, with pleasure pilgrims everywhere. The Jewish community had discovered the posh end of Brighton and its gin palaces. It had become the fashionable spot for long weekends and droves of families would arrive at the Metropole. The young girls wore the latest polished dirndl skirts under which swished petticoats of paper nylon. They wore colours that rocked the grey pavements: yellows, greens, oranges and azure blues. They looked vibrant and jolly. They wore dainty ballerina pumps and their dark heads were feathercut in boyish style, ears weighed down by bright coloured giant button earrings. Boobs were never higher, hitched up by those Maidenform bras. They promenaded the seafront, changed into glamorous boned bathing suits and vivid towelling bathrobes, only losing their poise when reaching the egg-shaped pebbles on the beach that turned their walk into a hunchbacked wobble. In the early evening the fun would begin again in the hotel's winter garden where dance bands played until late at night.

My ghastly Sundays became a wait for the festivities to begin. I would sit on the regal balcony over the front entrance of Auntie's hotel, my nose resting on my hands, and watch. Through the wrought iron balustrades the whirling skirts looked like umbrellas from above. I was sitting there in a donkey brown formal crêpe dress, peach lisle stockings and a row of little pearls, feeling like Cinderella. How could I ever be like those girls below? When it rained they all congregated at the glass entrance of the hotel. My only other diversion was to go on the West Pier and watch the poor escapologist, bound in chains, hurl himself into the spinach green waters. I almost wished he wouldn't come up, but he always did. I would flee before his partner could reach me with his hat, repeating over and over again, 'Don't forget the diver!'

We usually had tea upstairs, with sandwiches and cakes. I would sneak out and watch the tea dance from behind the glass door of the fire escape. They danced foxtrots, tangoes and waltzes between bites of creamy cakes, the ballroom dancing instructors swirling with willing pupils around the floor.

Upstairs Auntie was going through different fads. For consecutive Sundays we would learn how to make jewellery from beads and tassels, and when she grew tired of that hobby we would pass on to another. When she was tired of us she would send us to the news theatre with a holdall full of beautifully wrapped sandwiches, enough to feed a battalion. I was already looking like Bessie Bunter but Beatrice remained skinny as a rod.

I almost rebelled one blustery Sunday. I was made to wear Auntie's old sable coat and take my sisters to the ice rink. The fur coat reached down to my ankles and had my aunt's initials embroidered on the lining. To crown it all, I was handed a crocodile handbag that only a queen could hold with dignity. It was filled with sandwiches, all labelled, in separate damask napkins. I sat for two hours in my fur coat watching my sisters skate, wishing the ground would open and swallow me. Nobody I knew saw me, thank God, and my sisters enjoyed their skating afternoon.

My sisters were just as good at ballet, too. How I wanted to be a ballet dancer! We went to a local dancing school on the hill above Preston Park. It was full of budding cygnets and future go-go girls. I took ballet very seriously; I really had a feeling for it and I thought everyone could see how good I was. I practised hard in my room for the Grade One exam. Beatrice never practised. The moment came, and I was in the room alone with the two examiners. I had done all my steps correctly. I was so excited. I was going to be a prima baller-ina. The examiners watched Bessie Bunter thump around the floor, bumping against the bar, landing with great big thuds, swinging her huge piggy legs in all directions. When the lady at the piano stopped, Bessie took a few extra turns and curtsied and gave a great big Cheshire cat smile. I was *failed*, and struck off the list. Beatrice, of course, glided through like a swan.

I never went back to the ballet school on the hill. My aunt said I was ugly, and that my feet were abnormal. All this became part of the ritual of little talks with Auntie in the bathroom. Why did I look so sulky? Wasn't I grateful for all the things she was doing for us? I couldn't understand why Auntie was seeing us so much if we were such a burden. All the accusations usually came after lunch, during which my aunt drank endless glasses of soda water with a bit of lemon peel floating on the surface. It took many years for even my mother to realize those glasses were heavily laced with gin. I confused the smell with my aunt's perfume. To this day certain Guerlain scents remind me of gin and tonic.

Auntie was teaching us how to think, to breathe, to behave. She thought she was teaching us manners. She didn't realize that what she was really showing us was how to fight, how to strike, to retreat and strike again, how not to lose. She never lost. Right to the end she was winning. She lectured us on how the girls on the dance floor were vulgar. I longed to look vulgar and flashy. But when I had my freedom I reverted to those dull, sad, Auntie colours I had despised in my young days. They looked far better in England's grey light, almost vibrant against the grey buildings and pavements. Luscious, bright colours were meant for strong, sunny climates – for white pavements and clear blue skies.

On Sunday mornings before lunch we had lessons in ballroom dancing. The instructors, a married couple, were full of fun but I could never get those steps right. I studied the books with diagrams of black soles on the pages, showing how to do the steps. I could see those black footsteps all over the shiny parquet floor, but I couldn't get my feet to follow them. The whole thing was a shambles. How can you want so much to be graceful and elegant and yet be so clumsy?

By now I had become so shy I was almost unable to open my mouth. The words that did come out didn't seem to belong to me. I spent evenings tucked up in bed practising talking to people inside my head. I could talk very quickly and coherently to my imaginary friends but in reality I would become paralysed. Everything I said in front of my aunt she claimed was stupid, so the best thing was just to keep silent.

Auntie went through phases of golf and tennis. My sisters learned easily, but I kept getting sent off the tennis court and banned from the golf course. My first tennis lesson consisted of watching Auntie play with the hotel instructor. I watched her hit the ball, and saw the position in which she was standing. Never mind the instructor – he was to hit the ball to where Auntie had positioned herself to attack it. He was not to place any backhands or difficult shots unless she commanded him to do so, so it looked quite easy. But when I got on the court it was nothing like that: the balls kept whirling round my head and I couldn't hit a thing. The easiest way out was to close my eyes and just whack hard. Over and over again I was made to leave the court and watch Auntie's style. She couldn't have run to meet any shot in her mid-calf tailored skirt, with those peach lisle stockings under white socks, and tennis shoes. Her little clenched fingers were glittering with solitaire diamonds.

Auntie's next big fad was golf. I spent weeks of swinging that awful stick. I don't know who was more bored, me or the dwarf-like instructor. I remember falling asleep while I was on my hundredth swing. His report was dire and I was banned from the course. Beatrice, as usual, took to golf like a duck to orange. My only escape was to go to my room and read detective stories and daydream about film stars.

A television arrived. It was tiny, so Mother bought a magnifier which looked like a plastic fish tank filled with bubbles. Two big leather straps attached it to the back of the set. I spent the afternoons after school listening to crackling sounds and watching a picture that was like a few grey shadows darting now and then across the bubbling fish tank. But it was an escape from homework and those awful Sundays. All week I prepared myself for Sunday lunch. What would I say? What would I try not to blurt out? Would Auntie be in a good mood or was it going to be absolute hell? By Saturday the tension would become quite obvious. Mother would become loud and strained and by the time we had to climb the marble stairs of the gin palace my heart would be thumping and I would get a feeling that my head was wrapped in a sheet of gauze. By the time we reached Auntie's suite door I was virtually anaesthetized. We were to knock three times and walk in. One of us would have to be the first to walk in and sense the mood of the day. If Auntie was not in the drawing room we would all stand there mortified – we were too early. Auntie despised this as much as lateness.

One of the worst Sundays was my twentieth birthday in 1956, when my aunt handed me a large cheque. It sounds ungrateful, but I felt bought again. I would have to account for how I spent that money. I didn't feel like saving it or spending it – it seemed like a soiled cheque and was heavy in my pocket. When I deposited it I wrote out another one to the Hungarian Refugee Fund. The motive was wrong but I felt righteous. It was now my money and I could do what I wished with it. A month later, when my bank statement was examined by Auntie, I didn't feel quite so brave. I could see her trembling fury as she read the details of the cheque for £50 made out to the Fund. I myself was a refugee – how dare I send money to others?

One Sunday there was a newcomer. Aunt Sophie had bought herself a dog. He was the son of a champion Pekinese of the highest pedigree. He was perfect: a pale mousy blond with black streaky 'feathers', a flat nose and huge black eyes. He was a little bundle of fluff which turned in its middle years into a ratty, snappy little monster. He was christened Mr Poo after the dogs of Chinese emperors.

Poor Mr Poo never had the joy of sniffing all those lovely doggy smells on the Brighton seafront. After his paper nappy stage he was immediately introduced to the back corridors of the gin palace. At certain hours of the day, undetected by waiters and staff, my aunt and her maid, with Mr Poo on a lead, would sneak up the back stairs to the second floor and he would have a routine piddle in the back corridors. The maid, usually armed with a rag disinfected with Listerine, would remove the puddles. As children we were sometimes deputed to accompany the brigands on their mission, to act as lookouts for approaching strangers or floor managers. To make the expedition seem authentic the party had to wear coats and carry handbags to look as if they were about to visit friends. On the return to the suite Mr Poo's legs were washed and blow dried. On his birthdays he was allowed out on the strip of pavement outside the hotel as a special treat. When I come to think of it, I can't ever remember seeing a turd. His diet was of finest steak, weighed and cut up into weeny pieces with a special pair of silver scissors. He lost his teeth very early. Poor Mr Poo was programmed, just like the rest of us.

Auntie had been shopping for a title. There was no way a healthy blue-blooded man would marry a conspicuously foreign lady unless he was broke or homosexual, so she decided to buy herself status in life. She missed London and society. At the drop of a hat she would get on the Brighton Belle and travel to London for a lunch or tea date. One Sunday lunchtime she announced that she was going to buy a title and a country house as a sort of package deal. The problem was that the manor house she had in mind was in the depths of Northumberland. As we listened to her plans we became aware that we were included. I saw my mother's eyes roll back at the thought of being marooned in the country alone with my aunt. Many violent rows followed and Auntie, uncharacteristically, abandoned her plans.

My aunt always said she would only remarry if the man was a millionaire. After the war, there was a great shortage of men in general. The remaining few were either poor or well protected by their wives, so my aunt's social life revolved round other lonely women. She decided to throw her fortieth birthday party at the Ritz. My mother said it was actually her fiftieth but we were not to discuss this interesting conundrum. The lunch party was for fifty ladies and no men were invited. We children were dressed in taffeta frocks. I loathed mine, which was navy blue and had a million little pearl buttons on the front. For once my mother looked very beautiful in a grey silk full skirt and a little jacket to match. This displeased Auntie, who that day had somehow made herself look rather dowdy. Beatrice and I sat with our lips zipped as the fifty women were seated round the longest table I had ever seen. My aunt, who had positioned herself at the head of the table, looked tiny – dwarfed by rows and rows of women identically dressed in black dresses, pearls and white kid gloves. On top of each head was a bobbing flowered hat, swathed with veiling.

The relationship between my mother and my aunt seemed to deteriorate with each Sunday. During the week my mother lived in terror of her daily telephone talk with my aunt. At 6 o'clock each evening, not a minute earlier or a minute later, my mother would have to recount our day. There would be long silences while mother listened to reprimands. Sometimes, when the conversation ended, my mother would retire to her room in tears. Later she would take it out on us and tell us what my aunt had said: we were stupid, we didn't work hard enough. Mother spoiled us. When we were older we had to talk to Auntie each day as well as taking it in turns to dial first. To this day I cannot bring myself to dial even the closest of my friends. I have to get someone else to do it for me. But there were evenings when Auntie was in a good mood. Her cheerfulness would spread among all of us, and life wasn't really so bad after all. We took it in turns to be top of the pops. The favourite could do no wrong for a couple of weeks, but it wasn't long before you fell off the pedestal, and then the climb up again was very long and arduous.

It was difficult for a teenager to understand two adult sisters who spent all their time talking about each other with such venom and still remained together. My aunt seemed to revel in the power she held over my mother. I loved them both (although I certainly didn't realize at the time how much I cared for Auntie), and as I grew older could understand why sometimes there was no meeting point. My mother was weak but curiously stubborn. My aunt was just very overpowering. Everything she touched would bend the way she wanted it. If you were dependent financially on her, as we were, you could be cut out of the will; if you were a stranger, not yet caught in her web, you were a challenge which she had to overcome. The only person who seemed to stand up to her and to whom she listened was her lovely Scottish housekeeper. Jean Findlay, with her broad Scots accent, would calmly tell Auntie where to get off. It was a joy for us to hear her. She was devoted to my aunt but she told her quite openly she couldn't stand working for her for any length of time. Auntie's official companion, poor Mrs Bradfield, eventually had a nervous breakdown.

We were living on a ridiculous financial see-saw. One day we took the bus, the next day a chauffeured car. My mother always wanted a cottage with roses growing round the front door; my aunt would only settle for a castle. She wanted the best for us, or what she believed to be the best. My mother wanted to make sure we did not lose touch with reality or with true values. My aunt was a hard-bitten survivor and my mother simply existed. Which one of them was right? I couldn't tell then, and I'm still not sure.

Everyone around Auntie wanted to please her. The more they tried, the more she rebuffed them. As time went on, my sisters and I became more and more withdrawn. My mother still rebelled, but with less energy. We had been broken in. Any confidence and spontaneity disappeared. We came and went like zombies. Meanwhile my aunt went on with her daily routine but fewer and fewer friends came to see her. Her evenings were spent alone, even though she dressed in her tea gowns and jewels. She read, listened to the radio, and hit the bottle, too. The local dress shop would send new deliveries with a seamstress to my aunt's suite. Once they were summoned to show her formal overcoats for us children. I will never forget seeing the assortment of silk coats that were delivered, or the sick feeling in the stomach when I realized I was going to have to wear one of those monstrosities. Why couldn't we choose for ourselves? Maybe it was only an ordeal for me. My sisters seemed always quite happy and willing. Beatrice's coat was brown silk, a full-skirted coat dress, and mine was a revolting blue brocade with a huge shawl collar and an even more repulsive black velvet bow on the bosom. It was designed for a matron, not a fourteen-year-old. To crown it all I was made to wear one of those half-chewed hats that ladies wore then. I still can't stand having anything anchored on my head. It makes me feel trapped.

In that absurd attire we would set off on the Brighton Belle to London once a month. Once on the train I felt in another world.

Nobody I knew would see me looking so ridiculous. In London we would take a short walk through Bond Street and usually have lunch at the Coq d'Or, which is now Langan's Brasserie, the Caprice, Prunier's or Claridge's. Then we would explore the rest of Bond Street and go back to the Ritz for tea. Sometimes we went to Fortnum's. After tea it was back to Victoria Station to catch the 6 o'clock Pullman back to Brighton. Auntie was usually in quite a jolly mood on those days, so the journey was always fun. She could be marvellous at times, so I felt guilty about the days when I hated and feared her. But the next day her criticism would begin again. I would be told how I had been rude to some waiter the previous day, or how sulky I had been at lunch. My heart would sink. I just couldn't remember being rude to anyone, though perhaps I was. I thought I had been quite happy.

When I was fourteen Mother broke the news to me that I was going to be sent away to a real boarding school on the outskirts of Worthing. Maybe my marks and my manners would improve. Auntie had personally vetted the school and liked it very much. The fees were £86 a term, exclusive of extras, which was quite expensive then. Charmandean School was privately owned and there was no entrance exam. My reaction was of unqualified delight. I couldn't wait to be a boarder there, to have all those Enid Blyton adventures and midnight feasts. I was taken to Kinch and Lack to be kitted out with a brown tunic, tie and an amazing artichoke green rayon dress with a cream collar embroidered with three green dots on each flap. The coat was double-breasted pinky Melton and the hat was yet another vegetable green with a ribbon in the school colours. The school prospectus showed nymphets dancing in the woods. The gardens were littered with cement statues and young ladies sitting on horses. The booklet had not been revised since the 1930s and it was very Isadora Duncan. The school house was Georgian with wrought iron colonnades and on one side a massive winter garden. There was a circular swimming pool which looked like a small lake.

It was also a kind of St Trinian's. Miss Lotte West, the principal, rarely appeared except to take prayers in the morning. Miss Bunn was headmistress and her sidekick, Miss Cream, taught Latin and grammar. The school house was in grounds of 30 acres which had seen much better days. The grass tennis courts and the lawn where

Barbara Hulanicki on the
roof-garden at Big Biba in 1973
Desmond O'Neill

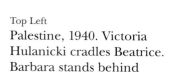

Top Left
Palestine, 1940. Victoria
Hulanicki cradles Beatrice.
Barbara stands behind

Top Right
Witold Hulanicki

Bottom Left
Barbara held between Aunt
Sophie (left) and her mother
at her christening in Jerusalem

Bottom Right
Victoria and Witold Hulanicki
on their honeymoon in Poland

Top
The winning designs in the
1955 *Evening Standard* fashion
contest. Barbara's beach outfit
far left

Evening Standard

Bottom
The original sketch by Rix and
fourteen years later an outfit
which appeared in the 1969
mail-order catalogue

Harry Peccanotti

Top Left
Felicity Green from the *Daily Mirror*, who gave us the kick-off

Top Right
Anthony Little, designer of the first Biba logo

Bottom
Church Street, Kensington

The dress that started it all

Top
Fitz and Barbara with some
of the original Biba girls
Courtesy of Bokelberg of *Storm* magazine

Bottom
Rosie Bartlett and Eva moving
to Church Street

Top Left
Moving shop. Cilla Black and Cathy McGowan helped move from Abingdon Road to Church Street in 1966
Syndication International

Bottom Left
First cosmetic unit at High Street Kensington Biba
S. K. Persaud

Top Right
Malcolm Bird's impression of the tea dance which launched Biba cosmetics. Twiggy dances with Witold on the left

Bottom Right
Art Deco logo for Big Biba
Designed by Whitmore/Thomas

Mandy Smith in the first Biba
catalogue

Donald Silverstein

the nymphets had danced in the sepia booklet were now overgrown. The statues had had their noses and private parts shot off by the soldiers who had used the house as barracks during the war. The circular swimming pool was only knee deep in water of a pea green colour, and its bottom was full of leaves. We had midnight feasts practically every night as there never seemed to be anyone to supervise us. We had a bath once a week, or when we remembered. It was heaven on earth, free for all. I loved every moment of that first term, after I had plucked up courage to open my mouth.

When I arrived I was shown my bed in the dormitory and there I stayed for the next six hours. I swung my legs back and forth and radiated my Esther Williams smile at everyone who deigned to look at me. The room held at least twenty girls. They all came and went but no one talked to me. I just sat there until it was obvious it was bedtime and I would have to make a move. I was paralysed with shyness.

After that first uncomfortable day, everyone was nice and friendly. I was put in a class with only three other girls: one fatty and a pair of blonde American twins. This class of four sounds as if it was something special, but it was actually because there were no more seats in the appropriate classroom, so they put the overflow into another little room. The fatty, luckily, was even fatter than me. The twins were as skinny as beanpoles and looked almost identical. They made me fetch and carry and I obeyed cheerfully. I was very impressed by them. They sulked when I got good marks. I was becoming oddly good at some lessons. Fatty wasn't bad but she was no match for me and the twins were way behind. This must say something about the academic standards at Charmandean. We were sometimes completely forgotten, since there was no teacher for us, but these little details did not bother us.

The school library consisted of a shelf of fifty books, most of which were Enid Blytons or *Film Fun* annuals left by former pupils. Our desks were filled with American comics brought by the twins. Their father was president of a big American company in London, their mother a languid beauty who did not work and worry for them as my mother did. They said she stayed in bed until 11 o'clock in the morning and this really impressed me. Their home was always being redecorated and they seemed to spend their holidays being chauffeured to parties. I wonder what happened to them. Their world seemed perfect and secure. How did they cope with the upheavals of later life?

At the time I wanted a twin. Now the thought of being stuck with your double for the rest of your life is horrifying. Close and large families have the same problem – the pain they have to carry for each other. Loneliness is sometimes more bearable than emotional responsibility for others. I never wanted to be involved with my family. The only person I wanted to be close to was my father and he was not there. I loved my aunt's strength and would have liked to have a part of it, but she was so destructive and dominating, she was frightened to allow anyone near her. I needed strong people. I fed off the twins' strength and they knew it. I loved my mother and sisters desperately, but they drained me. The twins were my first real friends in England. I know I was only their friend of convenience and they did not need friends because they had each other, but they strengthened me. As time went on my friends became less bossy and I began to find my own large feet. The long terms were a relief from the holidays which became more and more constricting. My aunt was becoming increasingly demanding and my Sundays now even more of an ordeal. After lunch the only thing we could all enjoy was listening to *Life with the Lyons* on the wireless. What a marvellous time they seemed to have. I wanted to have a real family like that. It took years to overcome it all.

But now I was starting to rebel against my aunt. School might not have taught me much, but I decided that I would be one person she would not crush. I remembered my father, who never gave in to her. At Sunday lunches I chose my words with great care, rehearsing them in my head first. I still felt Auntie could see into my head and hear what I was thinking, so I learned to concentrate on one subject. It was a good lesson to learn at an age when your mind wanders from one daydream to another. My dream in private was to be free and independent of Auntie. I longed for the day when I wouldn't have to account to anybody. I wouldn't have to say thank you to anybody unless I felt grateful. I wouldn't ever accept any emotional luggage from people because then I would immediately become their prisoner. I would never become like my mother. And if ever I was in the position of my aunt, I would give without demanding anything in return. I wouldn't accept any material things, either.

I missed my father so much that in a sense he was always with me.

He always helped when things were really bad. He was with me until I met my husband, and then he slowly went away. He still comes back when we are both in real trouble, and he still helps out.

Auntie must have been under financial pressure. Her own lifestyle was not cheap. She kept my mother and paid our school fees, but threatened to stop if we stepped out of line, or in fact if my mother did anything she disapproved of. I was terrified that my school friends would find out that it was not my mother who paid for me to be there; at the time it seemed shameful. It was actually because I had no father to foot the bills. I could never have my friends to visit me at home as the other girls at the school often did. I got on all right with most people at school, but I was still the odd one out. I was a foreigner and this was looked upon with suspicion. I remember being so ashamed when my surname was called out at roll call that I wished I could have a name like Smith or Jones. I mentioned this, one day, to Jean Findlay, my aunt's housekeeper, and I was amazed at her angry response. She said that there was one thing I had to be proud of and that was my father's name – it might be uncomfortable now but later it would be a great strength.

Chapter Four

My infatuation with South America began with the arrival at school of Christiana De Barros Conti. She was fifteen – much older than most of us – and tall, with a flowing mane of chestnut hair streaked with yellow tips. Christiana was suntanned and wore heavy tortoiseshell framed spectacles. She was well stacked, to the point where she found running most uncomfortable. She was nervy and highly strung, like a racehorse.

Christiana was as nutty as a fruit cake. Her world revolved around her mother's love life and her own numerous boyfriends. She had vowed to remain a virgin until she married, but she informed us that she would marry the first man who asked her. Fascinated, we sat round the common room listening to her amorous adventures, how men's 'trousers shook' as they looked at her. We were very naive – whatever did she mean? Our only knowledge of sex was picked up from girls who had brothers. I was brought up with hardly a man in sight, so I was terrified of them. My mother said that they were only after 'one thing'. The 'dirty papers', as my aunt called the *Sunday Mirror*, the *People*, and the *News of the World*, had articles on virgin births. My aunt warned us that she didn't ever want to hear of any virgin births at our home. She needn't have worried. I was so terrified and naive I thought you could have a baby by just thinking about it. I did wonder why Christiana hadn't had *that* problem since sex was all she ever seemed to think about.

On lazy sunny Saturday afternoons she and I would sit on the top rung of the wall bars in the gym while she told me about her romances in South America. While we chatted she nursed a bowl of peroxide on her knee and with a lump of cotton wool ran the foul-smelling stuff through her hair. She thought I should do the same with mine, so one day I dabbed a streak on top of my forehead. As the weeks and conversations passed, the streak grew to a whole lump and by the end of term I had a most odd blob of egg-yellow hair above my eye. Christiana said it really made me look much better. What Auntie said when she first saw me with that yellow cockade was unforgettable and unprintable. She made me dip my lump of bleached hair in a bowl of violet rinse. My hair turned purple, and we then tried to wash this out. We shampooed it for hours. I thought my hair would drop out. It was by now a pale blue. I could not go out for days and continued to wash it every couple of hours – eventually it turned a lovely ash blonde colour. Later, when I left school, I attacked the whole front part of my hair with peroxide. I've been blonde ever since.

As the years went by the happy schooldays turned tedious. I was growing up. By 1955, when I was just eighteen, the school had become more and more dilapidated. There was no money for repairs. Even fewer new pupils were enrolled and more and more girls left as they reached the fifth form. The school started to get that lovely musty, dusty look. As our numbers dwindled we all slept in one wing of the house. Big holes in the floor appeared, whole areas were cordoned off and made out of bounds. Some of the ceilings began to fall in.

Sometimes there were no meals. The two maids who were supposed to run the house did nothing all day and left in the evenings with huge carrier bags of food meant for us. One desperate night we were all so hungry that we went down to the kitchens to raid the pantry. It was bare but in the dustbin was lots of charred toast left over from breakfast, and we were hungry enough to eat it. When I told my aunt what was happening at school she said I was lying, but when I come to think of it, Beatrice never followed me to Charmandean. Beatrice was sent to St Mary's in Brighton. She was the brainbox of the family.

Later, in one of her very rich periods, my aunt decided to send Beatrice to Cygnet House in an effort to marry her off to a noble chinless wonder. Cygnet House was one of the last remaining polishing houses for rich young ladies before their debut into society. They went to endless coming-out parties and other social events, but my Cinderella sister found that the £3 pocket money, which had seemed a fortune in Brighton, was a pittance there, where silk couture gowns were the order of the day. The young future Aga Khan was not considered an eligible escort as he was not then the heir.

After Christiana De Barros Conti left, Vanessa became my best friend. She was very tall and aristocratic. By now the roll call in the mornings was very short as there were only twenty names to be called out. As we lined up, in order of age, the gaps could be dramatic. A ten-year-old girl was standing next to a fourteen-year-old. By such elimination Vanessa and I became the prefects to rule over eighteen girls. The sense of power was overwhelming. We each had a room to ourselves while the others were crammed into a couple of dormitories. The situation was so desperate that even I was asked to play the piano at prayers when Vanessa was ill. I was convulsed with laughter from trying to read music and playing with one finger. The choir was attempting to wail a hymn in time and it sounded like a cats' chorus. My report at the end of the term looked marvellous. I was games captain, prefect, and always either first or second in the class. Vanessa and I took turns. I was also in the choir and a note came from Miss Lotte remarking what a nice voice I had. In fact if things went well I could keep in tune to one bar, and I only bellowed in the parts I could cope with.

After my aunt read on my report that I was in the choir, she decided I was to become an opera star. She bought me a stack of sheet music and gave me several weeks to prepare myself to give her a recital. I was to learn 'Roses of Picardy'. I kept repeating faintly, 'But Auntie, I can't sing', and she would say, 'Yes, you can. Look at your report.' She had never heard me even hum. In collusion with Mother I managed to stave off the sing-song for six months, as the piano was in our flat and Auntie hardly ever left her suite.

Luckily, just in time Auntie found a new distraction, a tape recorder in a giant wooden cabinet. We used to have to read Dickens into it and then she would correct our diction, although her own voice was heavily accented. She sounded like Marlene Dietrich, but she was convinced that her English accent was perfect. On the other hand my mother could never complete a sentence in one language. She spoke English, French and Polish in one breath. I was unaware of this until I once saw one of my friends gazing at her in amazement, not having understood a word she had said.

When it was finally recognized that I was not going to become an opera singer, Auntie decided we should paint instead. Beatrice and I were to have art lessons in Brighton. I knew this meant drawing from life and I lived in absolute terror we would actually have to draw a nude. Every time the subject of the classes was mentioned I would blush and look away. Auntie must have realized what was bothering me, and called me into the bathroom. She explained that a nude wasn't really a nude when it was for art's sake. It didn't calm me down. When we actually arrived at the class, which was at the painter's home, I was shaking with fear. But the model came out in a most beautiful black satin bikini, and I was able, after all, to start to learn to draw.

My aunt wanted me to go to university, but I wanted to be independent and to earn my own money. I loved drawing and I loved clothes so I decided to say I would like to be a dress designer, which meant I could go to the local art school. At first my aunt was horror struck. Did I realize I would mix with people with long hair and dirty fingernails? My life up to now had been divided between a derelict building surrounded by green fields and a suite in a gin palace hotel.

My spare time was spent in the cinema. My horizon had broadened from Esther Williams to Nelson Eddy, Cornel Wilde, John Derek, and all the swashbuckling stars of the fifties. Jean Simmons was now my favourite. My aunt insisted that we should like Clark Gable, but I thought he looked like one of the waiters downstairs. However, Auntie won, and one Sunday we glumly professed our love for Clark and Maurice Chevalier – her other favourite. Most of the films I liked were harmless escapism or fantasy, but the time came when Auntie thought I should be allowed to see an 'A' film. The film was *All About Eve*, and I hated it. Bette Davis was physically too much like my aunt, but I loved the blonde in the last bit of the film – Marilyn Monroe.

Before my aunt would agree to my going to art school, she packed me off to Nice for four months to learn French. I was to stay with a lovely old dear, Mademoiselle Testue, who had been recommended by one of Auntie's friends. Before my journey I had sneaked out and bought a citron green blouse and huge matching plastic button earrings. For the journey I was wearing Auntie's old Donegal tweed suit but the blouse and earrings completely overpowered it. My suitcase was full of hand-me-down printed crêpe frocks and a heavy linen couture dress that Auntie had bought me. Mother had made me some lovely black shorts and rolled up in my towel lay a black, draped, Esther Williams-style bathing suit. My purse was bulging with £50 pocket money and I felt on top of the world.

Nice University was full of Swedish and other foreign students whose common denominator was some facility with English. After classes we would all go to the pebbly beach. I shall never forget the silence when I exposed my black draped bathing suit. All the other girls were clad in little bikinis. The only thing I could wear in Nice for the next few months were my black shorts and the citron blouse. At night I would embroider that pair of black shorts with a different stitch for each day, so it would look like I had a vast wardrobe of different pairs. If only Auntie could have seen how the local girls dressed! They wore little pastel coloured T-shirts with little matching shorts and beautiful leather Brigitte Bardot ballet slippers. My aunt would have said they were bad for my arches.

Those four months in Nice were magical. Mademoiselle Testue contacted the children of her family friends and we all went in gangs for picnics to beaches only the locals knew about, swam, snorkelled and sunbathed. In the evenings we went dancing at the cafés on the front. I fell in love with one of the boys but it was not reciprocated. When at last I got on the plane to go home my French was worse than before I had left, I had forgotten to collect my certificate for attendance at the university, and I had spent the £50 pocket money. One of my purchases was a pair of those beautiful ballet shoes. I had acquired a suntan, and my peroxided lump of hair was even more bleached. To cap it all I missed my flight connection in Paris. My aunt said I looked like a tart and that I behaved like a tart. For months I was reprimanded for having spent that £50 which, of course, would be worth more than five times that amount today. But it was worth all the furious repercussions to have seen the glamorous side of life for four months. Beatrice followed me a few years after. She came back with worse French than I did and had fallen in love with the same boy.

During the war Auntie's yacht had been requisitioned by the Italian Navy, and it had been destroyed by the RAF in a bombing raid. She had to return to England on the deck of a freighter, wrapped in her sables. Her companion on this journey was Somerset Maugham. Eventually she received compensation from the British government in the early fifties. After winning her case Auntie started to live really stylishly again. There were endless trips to London for fittings with Hartnell, Digby Morton and Maggy Rouff. She had wigs from Mr Teasy Weasy made to go with Mr Hartnell's sequined gowns. Those wigs were amazing. They were amongst the first to be seen in this country, made of nylon. They were hideous and resembled glossy swimming hats. At the end of a heavy evening the body heat would rise to her head, the wig would pop up and as she got tipsy the wig would end up at some rakish angle. But at least she was beginning to enjoy life again. She would disappear for a couple of weeks and return looking ten years younger after a facelift. The lisle hosiery disappeared and beautiful seamed stockings replaced them.

She bought herself the biggest diamond I have ever seen. She said it was yellow – that was why she could afford it. We received our precious gems education very early in life. Diamonds, Auntie said, should be bluish white not yellow, and set in simple shapes. Emeralds should be veined. Sapphires must never be too dark or too light, but a cornflower blue. Topazes must be a cognac colour and pearls should be light in weight and with no yellow hues. Thus all her friends' jewellery could be valued at a glance. With her wardrobe up to scratch Auntie discovered the *Andes*, a magnificent ship that was to become her home on and off for many years. She rarely disembarked, staying on from one cruise to the next regardless of where it was going. She slept through the day and emerged, sparkling, at night. Sometimes she was in the Mediterranean, sometimes the Pacific or Atlantic – it made no difference to her. On the early cruises she participated in all the activities and sightseeing tours. Other passengers might wear dresses and cotton T-shirts and shorts to go on shore, but my aunt would wear crêpe wool suits, high heels, veiled hats and kid gloves. She followed the bus in chauffeur-driven cars with her companion and perhaps some poor lonely passenger she had commandeered.

I was now even more determined to be free of my aunt. When you first spread your wings you gather too much fluff. You struggle to free yourself from home, and the next thing is you weigh yourself down by possessions and professional or personal commitments which eventually become your prison because you are scared of losing all those things full of memories. They are very hard to ditch once you are accustomed to them. You think you cannot live without them, but actually they are principally your padding and protection. Most people clutch them to their dying day, but some of us more fortunate ones who have been forced to step out have found an inner strength. I will never get weighed down by trappings again. My mother always drummed into us as children, 'Learn and learn: knowledge and experience is something nobody can ever take away from you. They can take everything material but not your mind.'

Despite my aunt's unease, she finally gave in and I enrolled at Brighton Art School in the middle of a course. Since Auntie had eventually calmed me about the idea of life classes, the shock of a naked body sitting there in front of a mass of people did not startle me except that this nude looked like a blob of suet pudding. My God, would I have to sit through two hours of trying to draw that mound of ugly flesh? I tried to avoid drawing the saggy tits and the bushy brush. I dreaded the moment when the lecturer would plonk himself by my chair and show me planes that I had missed, angles I was unable to see. When he eventually reached me he just mumbled, 'Christ, another fashion one', and that was the end of any guidance I got in life classes.

It was a relief to join the fashion class over the road with the Higher National Diploma students. Joanne Brogden was a visiting lecturer from London. She came down every Thursday and it was easy to work hard and to try and get praise from her. She lectured at the Royal College of Art and later became head of its fashion department. She never praised me but she certainly was a challenge. She made us draw and draw and she really aroused my interest. I looked forward to those classes. After a week of sketching Brighton Station, the Coin Exchange and those soggy nudes, they were a real relief. She also brought with her the spirit of a bigger, more interesting world. She was one of the best teachers I have ever come across.

As I was not a grant student, my aunt paid the enormous sum of three pounds and fifteen shillings a term for my tuition. As long as I signed in at the beginning of each session nobody ever said anything if I left the classroom ten minutes later, so I spent most of the next two years of art school in the cinema.

My social life revolved round art school jives on Saturday nights, but I had to leave at 10.30, just as everyone else was warming up and dancing to Bill Haley, Little Richard and Jerry Lee Lewis. My mother waited up for me to come home, so my love life was pretty mild. If I went out too often with one boy it meant I was 'at it' with him. My mother and aunt had embedded into me the thought that they were 'only after one thing' and this restricted my behaviour. At one Saturday night hop a group of dashing medical students arrived from somewhere in Surrey. Surely Auntie would approve! There was one I particularly liked. Some of my girlfriends and I went on with them to a club, but I was promptly ditched as I had to be home at eleven. I really liked that boy but he was a real 'rotter'. He took me out once or twice and that was it. I waited for his calls for months.

Auntie, after hearing about my being 'picked up' at the art school hop, decided to have a good look at the company I was keeping. She gave a dinner party on a Saturday night in the hotel ballroom where every Saturday there was a band. I asked the most respectable of my friends and I knew it would be a fiasco. There was Auntie in her 'silver fish' sequined Hartnell dress sitting at the top of the table, her wig getting more and more askew as the evening wore on. Amongst the guests were my girlfriends – off-beat Joyce, a six-footer in Greek beach sandals and a toga, who prided herself as a look-alike Marlon Brando. There was Pauline looking like Debbie Reynolds, and an architect friend wearing red socks and a dinner suit. I died a thousand deaths. There was not a drop of drink – that was Auntie's revenge. Nobody would ever come to her parties again, or mine, I feared.

One weekend in 1955 Auntie had spotted that the *Evening Standard* was running a design competition. There were three categories of entry: beach wear, day wear and evening wear. That afternoon Auntie made me draw and draw many times over a very strange dress that she had devised. It was a day travel garment – a combination of a printed silk dress with long sleeves over which you put on a linen wraparound skirt and then a linen jacket. The idea was that you travelled in the linen suit and peeled garments off as the day went on, finishing up in a silk dress for the evening. I was to draw in a straw hat with netting, gloves, pearls and a crocodile bag. I did what I was told and we posted Auntie's masterpiece.

The following day I entered the beach wear section. I did a drawing of a girl who was the image of Audrey Hepburn in *Sabrina Fair*. She was wearing a halter neck beach suit with little shorts. She wore those ballet pumps that ruin your arches, and huge dangling hoop earrings. I poured so much life into the drawing of that girl that one of the boys in the class came over and asked what her telephone number was and how he could contact her. *Sabrina Fair* had made a huge impact on us all at college; everyone walked around in black sloppy sweaters, suede low-cut flatties and gold hoop earrings. Few of us, though, could imitate Audrey Hepburn's skinny elegance.

One day I came back from college and Mother greeted me with flushed features and a telegram. I had won the *Evening Standard* competition in the beach wear section, out of three thousand entrants. I couldn't believe my ears. I was so excited I immediately phoned my aunt to tell her my good news. She was thrilled and said, 'You see, my dear, I know all about design.' It slowly dawned on me that she assumed it was her contraption that had won the prize. Meekly I confessed to her I had sent up a beach outfit of my own. There was a stony silence while she regained her composure. Immediately she began organizing the trip to London to collect my prize, which was a fitting with Hartnell to have my beach design made to measure.

I started to dread my appointment with Hartnell, where the other winners and runners-up were to meet. After a long battle not to wear another squashed hat with a veil, I turned up at Brighton Station in what I felt was appropriate, a beige duster coat. Auntie said I looked as if I was going on the beach. She, as always, looked beautiful and reeked of Guerlain's l'Heure Bleue. When we eventually arrived at Hartnell's, my aunt tried to take over the place. A very lovely blonde called Elizabeth Green, a feature writer on the *Standard*, had a moment of anxiety, but she was a match for my aunt. During the presentation Mr Hartnell made a quick appearance, took one look at the scruffy bunch of winners and promptly left. After being measured by a very snooty vendeuse with raised eyebrows, I joined my aunt and Miss Green for tea. As I stuffed another cake into my mouth Miss Green suggested I go on a diet. It had never occurred to me, nor my mother, nor Auntie, that in order to be sylphlike you couldn't stuff yourself with cream cakes.

My picture was in the *Standard*. I hated it and later lived in fear that someone would find the article in the library. When I received my winning beach outfit it was made up in stiff striped taffeta. I thought I would never get away from that ghastly fabric and now I was the proud owner of an 'evening' beach outfit! Polished cotton, which I had wanted, seemed to be taboo in couture circles. My aunt thought my beach suit looked quite nice. I gave her the Hartnell label to sew into one of her cheap little dresses for walking Mr Poo in the back corridors of the hotel.

In our second year of art school we all sat for our Intermediate exams. These were for the general course I was taking. The craft I was studying was fashion. In the sewing classes I had a sleeveless blouse that took two years to complete. For the exam I had managed to cut the pattern for a shift that consisted of two pockets, two darts and side seams. Pattern cutting drove me to despair but I was even worse at perspective drawing.

To everybody's astonishment I got through the Intermediate. Miss Brogden could hardly believe I had passed with my simple shift dress. After the exams I had to make a decision about choosing a subject for the next two years. For me it was either fine art or dress design. I couldn't face two more years of either painting or sewing so I decided to call it a day. I didn't tell my aunt, nor my mother, but wrote to a London studio that specialized in fashion illustration. My letter was very cheeky and very pushy. I had nothing to lose and the chance of avoiding going back to art school for another two years. To my shock and surprise, Helen Jardine Artists replied and asked me for an interview. I was so excited that when I dressed I put on my Young Jaeger grey suit back to front and never noticed until I came home waving a piece of paper saying that I had a job.

Mrs McLare, the proprietor, and Miss Hamilton, her partner, gave me a position as a trainee drawer, after looking at my portfolio full of Audrey Hepburn drawings. My job was to make tea, deliver the work of the senior artists to advertising agencies, and in between I could practise fashion drawing. I would be earning £5 a week. In addition I had £3 a week allowance from my aunt. I was beside myself with excitement: it meant I was almost independent and, what's more, I had one foot in London.

During my last year of art school I had become engaged. One long afternoon a group of us were sitting in a coffee bar, drinking endless frothy cappuccinos and listening to Johnny Ray singing 'Oh What a Night'. I had seen every film that week at least three times. We had exhausted our conversation about boyfriends, clothes, Audrey Hepburn and Marlon Brando when a friend from another college came in with two dashing naval officers. One was obviously her boyfriend, the other one had the widest grin I had ever seen. His name was Peter Dingemans. Suddenly the afternoon became exciting. The next evening he asked me to meet his family. There were Mrs Dingemans, Dr Dingemans, pretty Jenny, Baby Joe, firehaired Norman and Patrick. I had never seen such a happy family. Their rambling house stood on the edge of Steyning village. The doors were always open to everybody; friends, and friends of friends, drifted in throughout the day, patients called with presents, packs of golden Labradors romped around the house. The table was always laid for twenty or thirty in anticipation of whoever happened to appear. This was a new experience for me. Suddenly I was welcome any day and so were my mother and my sisters – even Auntie! But I was not going to let Auntie spoil this. By the time Auntie decided to have a look for herself, my terror of her disapproval had affected the entire Dingemans household. All week before her arrival we tidied up. Even the heaped billiards table was cleared of magazines, books, tennis racquets, coats and scarves. The cushions were puffed up and the rugs straightened. Eventually Auntie arrived like the Queen of Sheba in her chauffeur-driven car. She swept in, sparkling with diamonds and sporting a cheeky veiled hat. I could see even she was infected by all that happiness. Her eyes were twinkling, and she almost smiled.

I was very proud of Auntie that day. She behaved like a trouper when the bare spring in the squeaky floral sofa battled with her suspender. Auntie was human after all. Two weeks later, Peter and I got engaged.

With new strength I attacked my career with concentrated energy. My life (being married to the Navy) was going to be an upheaval of long goodbyes, so now my independence was even more important to me. My drawings were getting better and I seemed to get more time to practise between the delivery trips to a small agency in Swiss Cottage and making tea twice a day.

I was now off Audrey Hepburn and into Grace Kelly. By now my hair was longer like hers, bottled blonde and wavy, and I searched the shops for an ice pink twinset like the one Grace wore in *High Society*. I dreamed of being a debutante with a palace presentation and coming-out dance. I wanted to be a plump deb in a pale blue net crinoline with chinless wonders fighting for my favours. As I boarded the commuter train in Brighton I would plan my 'season's wardrobe' but by the time I had reached Victoria the dream would have to fade. Grace Kelly, having trudged up the hill at Charing Cross tube station and reached the fruit market in Covent Garden, had all her dreams shattered. Grace turned into Cinderella again as she climbed up the five flights of steps smelling of rotting vegetables to the attic of the studio. In the room where I dreamed of ice blue, flowing, strapless ball gowns sat Susan, another illustrator, whose idol was Greta Garbo. The wall behind her desk was covered with photographs of Garbo as Queen Christina, Ninotchka, Camille and the badly maltreated Marie Walewska. Susan sat there looking tragic all day, while I was sur-rounded by imaginary floating tulle.

To get yourself clad in something nice then seemed virtually impossible. Wallis sometimes had the odd simple black dress and they were usually designed by Sheila Camera. I could just pick out her clothes from all the others, they were so perfectly simple. I had found a most beautiful black wool dress with transparent chiffon sleeves by Just Jane and designed by Jean Muir. But these odd pieces were far and few between. One day as I was driving down the Kings Road I noticed a new shop. The windows were filled with panels on which were pinned dresses, blouses and skirts. I couldn't believe my luck. Not only was there one simple black dress with no nasty buttons or detail, but the rest of the clothes were equally simple. I immediately went and bought the black dress, which was 20 guineas – a fortune in those days. I hadn't even noticed the name until I left carrying a bag with Kiki Byrne printed on it. I introduced the shop to Susan, who went berserk and bought one of everything. We both earned quite a lot of money, but by the time we left the shop we were skint. Kiki Byrne never got the recognition she deserved.

The first signs of fashion that came from the street and not from the couturiers were starting to appear. At 1 o'clock each day there were queues in the Strand outside the Lyceum for lunchtime danc-ing. As time went by the clothes or the girls became more and more exaggerated. Their hair was now backcombed into a tall cone on top of their heads. They hobbled in their tight pencil skirts and on shoes with stiletto heels and the most vicious pointed toes. Those toes became as exaggerated as the bouffant hairdos. The boys wore early versions of mod suits and shoes equally pointed, made by Stan in

Battersea. Everyone flocked to have custom-built shoes. When Fitz and I were first married we used to go down there to watch the crowds ordering their specials. Some of the pointed toes were 8 inches long. Stan had a marvellous photograph on the wall of a couple dancing, both wearing shoes with toes like sabres. The girls were all immaculate and identical. We were told they bought their clothes from C & A.

I had become completely engrossed in fashion drawing. The idea of becoming a designer had been ditched: it was far too difficult. At first you would have to pick up pins in couture establishments for years on end. You might then be lucky enough to progress to sewing a few dresses. I couldn't see myself sustaining the interest. Drawing was an instant way of seeing results. It improved with hours of practice. It was important to simplify everything for printed reproduction, as the more bold and uncluttered your drawings were, the more chance there was of selling them. Even more important was the drawing of the head, which usually defined your style. From childhood, when we used to make Mother sit and draw faces for us, I had always liked drawing faces best. It took many attempts to get the right expression into the eyes. It had to happen instantly, like tying a bow, otherwise it looked too laboured. Some days you can get a perfect bow the first time you try, other times it can take ages to get a nice shape. Your own mood of the moment is also essential. If you are feeling angry you tend to draw angry faces. When you feel depressed, miserable faces keep appearing on the paper. I found I could draw best at 4 o'clock in the afternoon when I felt most relaxed. I would draw as many faces as I could between four and five, when it was time to pack up and go. The following morning I would struggle with drawing their bodies and hands, which I hated.

The worst part was the actual clothes. The garments that were sent into the studio to be illustrated were horrendous. I had to draw young bodies wearing dreadful trousers and try to make these monsters look well cut. Other clothes were badly shaped. Armholes were halfway down to the waist with no sleeve head, so you couldn't even lift your arm. Such clothes were designed for lumps. My designing frustrations were satisfied by trying to make the collars and the funny shaped sleeves look as nice as possible. No one seemed to know how to cut in those days. The only decent clothes were French. The young then were buying Dutch clothes from C & A and having them altered to fit better. For me *Elle* magazine was the bible.

I had progressed from advertising to editorial work. This did not pay as well but it was important to me as my portfolio was building up. The studio operated on a freelance basis. I signed myself just Hulanicki, as it sounded like a man. It was always men who seemed to reach the top, not women. At first I thought men would only deal with men, but I soon realized there were very few women who persevered with a career.

I moved on from drawing for *Homes and Gardens* to *The Times*, the *Daily Express* and *Woman's Mirror*. My ambition was to work for *Queen*, whose layouts were fantastic. Mark Boxer was art editor and Annie Trahearne was fashion editor – one of the nicest people to draw for and full of infectious enthusiasm. In England only *Queen* used print images in an interesting way. I drooled over Donald Silverstein's pictures, taken with a special lens where the heads were in enlarged foregrounds and the rest of the body seemed to disappear to minute proportions. The most beautiful face to draw from photographs was Ros Watkins, who would pose with her head down and eyes raised straight into the camera.

I drew for Prudence Glynn on the *Woman's Mirror*, which became very important to us later in the early Biba days. I was terrified of Jill Butterfield on the *Daily Express*. She was one of the most exciting journalists of my generation. I would never miss her page on Mondays. She usually used marvellous photographs with drawings. Another terrifying lady was Mary Delane on *The Times*. Barbara Griggs on the *Evening Standard* was lovely to work for.

Max Maxwell on *Vogue* was a very inspiring art editor. He started me off drawing from Alphonse Mucha posters – very elaborate Art Nouveau drawings. I even had a spell of drawing 'Mrs Exeter' for *Vogue*. She was an imaginary fortyish lady. My heart was not in drawing ladies of this age group, so I was soon dropped. Liz Dickson was fashion editor of the then frumpy *Tatler*. She was using great photography and when she did use drawings to illustrate features she would give me pages and pages to fill. Once when she was pushed for a story she had me photographed in clothes of my choice.

I spent many years working for the London office of *Women's Wear Daily*. This was the most interesting job of them all as I went to cover social occasions, and visited private homes to draw society ladies in the ball gowns they were going to wear that evening. I drew at private and very secret previews of the wedding dresses of the Duchess of Kent and Princess Alexandra at John Cavanagh, and saw other royal ladies at Hartnell and Hardy Amies. The star model at Amies was Sue Lloyd, who later went into films. When the London collections came round twice a year I would trudge round the fashion houses to despatch a daily drawing to New York. The most prominent and popular designer then was Michael at Carlos Place. His collections were very beautiful and elegant.

After one showing, John Fairchild of *Women's Wear Daily* gave me a long ticking off. I was not to lose the concave look of the jackets when I drew. At that time underfed mannequins would walk with their heads forward, shoulders well back and hips pushed forward with a deliberate concave curve of the chest, gliding forward and dragging a very expensive fur behind them on the floor. Their little heads were planted on swan necks, their expressionless faces caked with orange panstick and their hair scraped back into chignons. They were but skin and bone and however much I dieted I always felt like Bessie Bunter, so maybe that's why I fleshed them out a bit in my drawings. Envy! After a show I felt I looked like a country bumpkin next to all that sprayed elegance.

Fashion in the late 1950s was definitely for thirty-year-olds and over. I was looking forward to the day when I would be that old and able to cope with all the elegance. I imagined myself being sketched for a change, wearing three rows of pearls and a black chiffon dress. I still wasn't quite sure if I would look like Grace Kelly, Audrey Hepburn, or maybe Greta Garbo.

I had discovered that if I ferried myself to Paris at my own expense, I would always be able to sell drawings to some publication. I was never able to get seats for the first shows but somehow, someone from the press would get me a ticket to the second or third showings of a few of the couturiers. The Christian Dior show was still the most sumptuous and forceful, although the genius himself was dead. There were Nina Ricci, Lanvin, Chanel, Guy Laroche, Pierre Cardin, and Balmain, where Ginette Spanier reigned.

The day after a show I would be given a number and description of a dress to sketch by the fashion editor. I had to go to the fashion house and get past the press officer to see the dress, and then persuade a model to put it on so I could sketch it. At first I was nervous, trying to remember all the details. When eventually a very bitchy model would deign to put the garment on, she demanded the modelling fee before she would place herself in a pose. Then with moans and groans she would stand there swaying backwards and forwards. I was terrified of taking more than a few minutes. I later discovered that other illustrators sometimes made them stand still for hours. I would be shaking and the model would be swaying and fidgeting, so later in the evenings in my grotty little hotel room I tried to recreate in my mind what I had actually sketched. Little did I realize at first that the exhausted fashion editor would have seen at least two thousand garments that week and was relying on me to jog her memory about what she had thought important at any particular show.

The superstars of Paris, Balenciaga and Givenchy, did not show with the rest of the mob. They would usually show a month later, which meant that the whole press corporation would have to troop back to Paris. To make life even more difficult the fashion houses set an embargo on publication within two months after the shows. Only the elite were ever allowed to see a Balenciaga show. In all the years of toing and froing to Paris I never managed to see one. I even tried being ostentatiously Polish with the Polish woman who ran their press office. Nothing doing. I was allowed to sketch only three or four garments on the request of an appropriate publication. In my heart of hearts I really couldn't see what everybody was raving about. I thought Balenciaga's things were old, heavy, and too structured to be worn; at any rate the dresses I was asked to sketch seemed to be. He lacked any humour, but I suppose Paris fashion has no humour.

I much preferred his partner in crime who resided on the other side of the road. Givenchy's clothes were pretty, delicate, young and, most important of all, my idol was dressed there. Audrey Hepburn and Givenchy were made for each other. His little black dress with shoestring straps in *Sabrina Fair* must have been imprinted on many teenagers' minds forever. I was out of my mind when I discovered at one showing that she was coming to choose her wardrobe for a feature in *Vogue*. I was the first to arrive and planted myself towards one side of the front row. I switched a fashion editor's card to another seat – nothing would budge me. I sat there defying any snippy snotty vendeuse to move me from my seat. The elite from French *Vogue* seated themselves around two thrones set up for Audrey Hepburn and her husband Mel Ferrer, and the rest of the press ladies balanced on the most uncomfortable rickety gold chairs. We waited for the royal couple to arrive.

At the appropriate moment, when everybody had been seated and before the fidgeting started, Audrey glided in. She was lovely, but she was human. She was huge – her feet were bigger than mine! Her proportions were exaggerated. She was like a fashion drawing brought to life – huge eyes, mouth, and quite a large nose, too. Her head was small with a little pillbox hat balanced on the back of her crown, her doe eyes framed by heavy raised eyebrows had the expression of a gazelle about to take a leap. Her neck was like an exaggerated drawing. Her torso was long, flat and concave and she held a little crocodile bag dangling on a gold chain. She had long muscular legs but moved like a ballerina, wearing those coveted low-cut black suede pumps on a miniature heel. It was the first time I had seen an idol in real flesh. She was a human being like the rest of us, with a few bumps and lumps, not all of them in the right places, but she was exceptional. I almost wished I hadn't seen her in the flesh. It broke the magic on celluloid.

Evenings in Paris were an anticlimax. I stayed in second-rate hotels around the Champs Elysées, handy for the following day's work. After the daily tension and hassle I would retreat to my depressing hotel room and gorge myself on crispy French bread, creamy white butter, cheese and sausage. I assumed all the press ladies were having a marvellous time partying and dancing or going to night clubs. I was almost as terrified of them as I was of my aunt.

After each trip to Paris I felt I'd never be asked to do another job. I suppose that is the usual insecurity of a freelance.

The shops in England at this time were full of matronly clothes – either direct copies of Paris models or deeply influenced by the Paris collections. There was little specially designed for the young. I used to covet the clothes the twins, with whom I was still in touch, were sent from America. The contents of their cupboards could have filled a shop. Circular gingham skirts, marvellous stiff paper nylon petticoats – what made their wardrobe even more exciting was that they always wore identical clothes, so there was a duplicate of everything. It was their shoes I envied most. They were the simplest pumps, very low-cut to show what used to be called toe cleavage. I longed for similar shoes. I walked the main street of Brighton studying shoe shop windows for hours. Maybe there was a pair of those simple pumps hidden in the monstrous displays of hundreds of left feet. I found a pair. Hooray! They were almost the right shape but my toes didn't show. I bought them anyway and attacked them with a razor blade to cut out part of the front of the shoe. While I was trying to make the other shoe match, my mother came in. She was forever catching me cutting off bows on Auntie's hand-me-down dresses, but never before on shoes. My bedroom was a hospital of half-made dresses. Eventually Mother would take pity on me and finish the dress for me. She would grumble as I made her squeeze the waist too tight, so that of course it split at the first movement.

Another of my home industries was to mix my own foundation, as the only colour you could buy then was bright peach. The peach paste you applied to your face would leave a frame around your forehead and chin, so I would add some white poster paint and a big blob of ochre gouache paint. It seemed to work very well and I used it for years until one day someone told me I was lucky to have any skin left as the paint contained an awful lot of arsenic.

My aunt and I were not getting on. She had lost control of me. I had become independent financially very quickly, earning an awful lot of money for someone of my age. Her allowance was a pittance. I sound churlish and ungrateful, but for me this self-possession was a triumph. I was the only one of my family who did not have to listen to her nonsense. I even found the courage to fake something more important to do on a Sunday and miss one of those tortured lunches. Soon I could afford to leave home and live in London and buy myself a car.

In between trips to Paris and drawing corsets for catalogues and commuting up and down to Brighton I would see Peter. He was away most of the time in Portsmouth, Malta and other exotic places. The reunions were happy and very romantic – at naval balls and parties on submarines. But we were only building a store of memories of fleeting tearful rendezvous and farewells, and one time in Malta I found myself sitting on a beach with six women looking out to sea. Three of them were pregnant, the other two plotting and planning their next meeting with their husbands. I thought I couldn't spend my life homeless and looking out to sea. I wanted to live in big cities and not to travel with my home in a few suitcases.

My aunt was furious with me when I broke off the engagement. I was twenty-one now and she thought I was getting a bit long in the tooth! My sister Beatrice had married her first love, Tommy, in spite of my aunt's efforts to find a nobleman for her, and she went to live in Ghana with him. Only Biba was left with Mother and Auntie. Their full attention was centred on her, poor thing!

By this time, in the early 1960s, my aunt was living between the Metropole and the *Andes*. She only disembarked to return to the gin palace for a brief change of wardrobe. She still lived by the 1930s' fashion rules. On 1 September her straw hats were carefully stored in boxes and the felts were unpacked. Sometimes there was time to have them remodelled into more fashionable shapes. When all the necessary arrangements were finished, a convoy would embark on the journey to Southampton. A few paid-for guests would accompany her, followed by a van containing her wardrobe and her secret bar – crates of gin packed into trunks.

In 1960 my mother was at last persuaded to join her on a particular cruise around the world. It meant two months of concentrated Auntie. My aunt was generous when she was rich. She lavished my mother with Hartnell and Maggy Rouff evening dresses, and over the years she had given her many lovely pieces of jewellery that had become too subdued for her as she was now into Taylor-size rocks. When they reached Southampton and my aunt's luggage was unloaded, the two porters could not lift her trunk full of Gordon's gin. A crane had to be found. It was a memorable cruise for my mother – her life began again. She met Humphrey, whom she was later to marry, on that voyage. They were together for eighteen years until she died. Mother became beautiful again, aged forty-four and in love. Auntie was furious. On their return Mother was longing for Humphrey to contact her. When he phoned her she was euphoric. He had asked to meet her in London, but she thought she couldn't possibly stay the night. He must be after that one thing! Her three daughters staunchly advised her that it was perfectly above board for her to stay in London, at her age. She went to London and we lost our ever-loving Mum to Humphrey.

In 1960 I was twenty-three and, in Auntie's parlance, on the shelf. I had a married younger sister, and my sister Biba was only fifteen, so she was still in the clear. At the studio I sat and listened to Susan's adventures. She shared a flat in London and spent every night going to parties and living a boisterous life. She and her brother Nick seemed completely wild. I would listen to her tales with amazement. In many of their escapades a man called Stephen Fitz-Simon, always known as Fitz, seemed to be included. I felt I knew them all personally.

I had to break away. I had commuted from Brighton for two years and I had had enough. Jenny Dingemans, Peter's sister, found a flat in Douro Place and the two of us, with two other friends of hers, moved in. The novelty was exhilarating until one became too familiar with one's flatmates' habits. There were rows about cooking and cleaning – the only time we would all join ranks was when a party was organized. It was at one of these parties that I first saw Fitz.

The minute I saw him it was as I had hoped it would be. I had seen it so many times in films and I was quite sure that one day it would happen to me. He was the worse for wear, propping up a cupboard with a glazed look in his eyes, occasionally swaying forwards and then regaining his balance. I said to myself, 'There's trouble, but he's the one for me.' He had found our secret reserve of drink and drunk it all, and he was being bullied out by my flatmates. That was the last I saw of Fitz for a couple of very painful years.

The rest of the evening seemed to be monopolized by someone called David. He asked me to have lunch with him the following day. At that lunch he asked me to marry him and by the time we had coffee I said, 'Yes.' It was a very strange feeling of not being in control. I told my aunt on the telephone the same day. She said, 'He's a Jew – how can you marry a Jew?' I told David he was a Jew. David said it was the first he'd heard of it and he'd ask his mother – but did it matter? His mother said he wasn't Jewish. My aunt still insisted he was. I didn't care. I was immediately cut out of the will.

The following Saturday David and I set out after lunch, in his new car, to go to a party in Brighton and to meet my mother and aunt. It was David's first car and he hadn't driven much before. As we went through Croydon I fell asleep. When I woke up I was vomiting into a bedpan. I was lying in a hospital bed. I felt very sick and my eyes could hardly focus but I heard a voice saying to me, 'Barbara, don't you remember me?' It was the 'rotter' medical student from art school days. Why weren't they saying anything about David? They were all joking about the expensive lunch I must have had. As my eyes came into focus and I said, 'Where's David?' they said not to worry, he had been taken to another hospital. Why another hospital? Why not the one I was in? Because he was unconscious, they said, and would receive better help there.

Two weeks later, when I was discharged, David was still unconscious. The week before my aunt had visited me. She told me, 'Surely you can see it's God's will?' I couldn't think. I had known him for so little time before being plunged into this crisis. I could hardly remember his features. I forced myself to recall details about him. My aunt continued the attack. She told me I had to come on a cruise with her. I hated my aunt – the last thing I wanted was to go away. I couldn't wait to go and see David and try and wake him. She said he would never wake again, but I knew he would. He was far too strong to give up. When David awoke he did recognize his mother. I immediately drove down from London to see him. He didn't recognize me. At intervals he improved and one day he 'recognized' me. He said, 'Hello, you're the pubkeeper's daughter.' I cried because the tension had been so intense. The nurse was nice. She said it was because he had not known me for very long and it took time for the brain to catch up with time and later he would remember.

If our bonds had been deeper I would have married David then and I was determined to do so once he was out of hospital. My life revolved around his sick bed. I visited him three times a week for eighteen months. I would drive to the hospital full of hopes of a fragment of improvement. Sometimes I would come back crying, occasionally elated beyond belief because I had seen some spark. Sometimes these flashes were there for more than a split second and I thought there might still be a happy ending for us. At first I was completely determined to devote my life to looking after him. I earned enough money to get by for both of us. After all, I now had a flat of my own and was completely independent.

My aunt stopped my allowance as the last threat. I had stuffed my ears so I couldn't listen to her any more. My mother couldn't help. I had to work this out by myself. I was tormented by my conscience and my own sense of survival. As time went by, David as a person became more and more unreal. The pubkeeper's daughter became an enemy. I was emotionally exhausted. There was no progress, and as his physical state improved he was moved to a hospital with locked doors. I took him for walks in the gardens, after which he joined the other patients and the doors were locked again.

Eighteen months after the accident I went to visit Beatrice in Ghana. I contracted measles, hoped I would never recover, got drunk, cried until I was dry, and vowed never to see David again.

Chapter Five

When I returned to England I was living alone in Cromwell Road. One evening I decided to go and visit my former flatmates in Douro Place. Later, as I was nattering to the girls, there was a phone call for me. There was heavy breathing and an awful voice like an old man's started rambling muddled obscene things to me. I got really scared. How could this man have found the address of my old flat? If it was that easy, surely he would just find my flat in Cromwell Road and come and murder me? But the girls in Douro Place were getting pretty sleepy, and I had to go home.

When I entered the hall I couldn't face going up the flight of dark stairs, so in desperation I woke up Mr and Mrs Joseph, who looked after the house and lived in the basement. I asked Mr Joseph to come upstairs with me. While I was blurting out my story to them the door-bell rang. Mr Joseph picked up a heavy spanner and crept up the stairs.

There at the front door was Fitz, asking if he could come up and see me because he had heard that my flat was for sale and he wanted to buy it, as he was shortly getting married. He was very persuasive and we sat down and discussed how quickly I could move out. All I could feel was envy that he was making all these plans for someone else. I even threw in my new fridge for nothing. By the time Fitz left I was feeling really cross. Not only was he getting married but he'd also broken my new sink cabinet. I had offered him some sherry in a giant tumbler and he sat on the draining board to drink it. The whole cabinet came away from the wall.

I didn't see Fitz again until Susan's mother gave a Christmas party. He was there with his fiancée. I was madly in love with him. We got on like a house on fire and never seemed to stop laughing together. A few weeks later he asked me to dinner. It was the beginning of a short and stormy romance. It just felt right emotionally. At last I could stop looking over my shoulder.

I wasn't sure I could cope with this confusing romance, and agreed to go to New York with Mary Potter, an American who was staying in my flat. The weekend before I left I asked Fitz to come to Brighton and meet my mother. She cooked lunch, Polish meatballs, and Fitz always said that he really fell in love with me then. He assumed I could cook like that, but the truth only came out after our honeymoon. He didn't know he was destined for a life of cold baked beans.

That afternoon we went for a walk on the seafront and he proposed to me. I said 'No' and continued with my plans to go to America. Mary Potter and I sailed from Southampton on a German ship. As it sailed into the Solent the band on board was playing 'Auf Wiedersehen' and there was Fitz on the quay getting smaller and smaller. I nearly jumped overboard to swim back to shore. The voyage was ghastly. Why was I going in the wrong direction? By the time we reached the mid-Atlantic I was missing Fitz terribly, so I climbed up to the ship's radio room and telephoned him. He still loved me and begged me to get a plane home as soon as I arrived. I said my mother would kill me and that I would have to stay at least a week in New York.

The seas had been so rough that the journey took an extra two days. But, now that I knew I was going back to Fitz, all the agony was worth it for the first sight of New York. The ship slowly sailed in at dawn, with a pink sky behind the Manhattan skyline. My big dream had always been to see America and here I was, but all I really wanted to do was to go straight back home.

I spent some lovely days in New York and Connecticut with Mary's family. Fitz and I corresponded daily. Mary and I spent lots of time at the Piping Rock Club where Mary's Grandma had a house in the grounds of the golf course. I felt sure that Bing Crosby and Doris Day would appear at any moment. I loved it all and thought it would be nice if Fitz and I could live in America. Fitz had a marriage licence ready and we were going to take the plunge as soon as I returned. I wrote to Mother with the good news. I felt strong enough to face the family fireworks. Auntie had disowned me but I was still anxious for her approval. When I flew back from New York Fitz was there at the airport, but I scarcely recognized him. He looked like a matchstick, he had lost so much weight.

My upbringing didn't allow me to live with a man, so it had to be marriage. Had we been a few years older we would have lived together and not got married, which would have been more of a challenge. I would like to have known that challenge, to live with Fitz knowing I could walk away at any moment.

We had been together for only six weeks and it dawned on me later that all our near ones and dear ones were assuming it was a shotgun wedding. They had a long wait to see the shot, as our son Witold wasn't born until six years afterwards. All we wanted to do was get married quickly and with no extravaganza. I was going to wear my favourite dress, which was splattered with red poppies. Mother was horrified. She said red was unlucky. She dragged me round the shops to see if we could find a better dress. Eventually after an unsuccessful day we bought some off-white silk and a *Vogue* pattern and poor Mum sat up all night making it. I refused to wear anything on my head, but was made to change my mind and wear a hat at the last minute. I loathed all that conformity.

We were married in November 1961 in a side chapel of the Brompton Oratory. Fitz turned up, to my surprise; now he says he was surprised to see *me* there. At the wedding, on my side of the church there were only my mother, my two sisters and my brother-in-law. On Fitz's there were his parents and his sister, Auntie Margie, and best man Andrew. Our wedding was so nice that I half wished we'd had a huge celebratory marriage. Fitz's father paid for the wedding feast as Mother was too frightened to ask Auntie to help out.

The newly wed Mr and Mrs Stephen Fitz-Simon set out on their honeymoon to St Ives, in Mrs Fitz-Simon's red Mini, since Mr Fitz-Simon's car, an MG, was a trifle unstable. The door handles were tied on with bits of string. Fitz had wanted us to go abroad but I had had enough of travelling and wanted to stay in England.

I don't know what it is that makes me so nervous in the country. The more nervous I am the more I eat. By the time we reached Land's End I had gorged myself with dozens of Cornish pasties. As we looked over the edge of the cliff I threw up – Fitz said I held the record for the most westerly puke in the British Isles. He promised me that one day he would buy me that rock to commemorate our honeymoon, but when it did eventually come on the market in 1981, it cost £10 million. It is now a caravan site.

All my life I had been suffering from a lack of confidence in my own identity. As soon as I became close to anyone, my family, my friends, both male and female, my strength and self confidence drained until the claustrophobia became too much for me and in desperation I would run away. With Fitz it was completely different. He did not make me feel vulnerable. With him my strength increased. He made me feel that I could be rational in any emotional situation without feeling guilty. He drummed into me that I shouldn't enter a situation feeling in the wrong. I must feel that I am right and everyone else is wrong. I could never master that confidence after the years of being undermined by my aunt. With Fitz I could get on with my work, to him I was always right and no one should ever undermine my judgement.

After we had got over the hump of adjustment and began to think as one, life began to take a new perspective. Every disaster turned into a funny story. We could twist events to see them in a different light. Had I been alone I would have seen it through melancholic Polish eyes; now I was looking at everything from an Irish angle too. The Irish and the Poles seem to be two lunatic nations that are completely compatible.

I had my drawing and he was an account executive in advertising. Together our income was substantial and with a new confidence and security I decided to leave the studio and go freelance. At first I remained with Helen Jardine as my agent. I had been at the studio for three years and as much as I loved the two ladies I wanted to leave the cosy atmosphere. I soon fancied myself with a tougher agent, one who would get me better fees for advertising work. My new agent, Mr Knight, had at least one curious claim to fame; he had refused to handle *Peyton Place*, on the grounds that it had no literary merit.

Like any other newly married couple, Fitz and I had to adjust to each other. When he came home from work he found me ready to go out on the town. He wanted to put his feet up and I had been alone drawing ghastly corsets all day and could not stand another moment in the flat. His evening meals with me were usually out of a tin, with an occasional lovingly mixed burnt omelette, for which he was most grateful. He was always given a choice; food that didn't generate much washing-up, or a hurricane in the kitchen. We could both see we were on a collision course, so I was desperate to try and find something we could do together. At first he was not convinced, but it was

becoming obvious we would have to do something where our energies could be united. I felt more and more strained about this.

One day Fitz came home and said I should design some garment.
He thought we should try and sell it by post. Although we both
earned a lot, we had no capital, so Fitz decided that if we could sell by
post, we could receive the payment with the order, before we had to
pay anything out ourselves. It was risky, because if anything went
wrong we had the responsibility, but at least we had the chance to do
something. I had a very strong hunch about an inexpensive long
evening skirt. It was just a long tube with a drawstring. Joanne
Brogden, who was still teaching at the Royal College and whom I'd
kept in touch with, came to our aid and found us students to make up
a sample. Fitz then took the skirt to Jill Butterfield on the *Daily Express*
who, to our delight, was thrilled by the price, 2 guineas, and said she
would feature it.

Fitz and I went home, got tiddly and tried to think of a name for
the new venture. We were so excited about it, we really believed our
fortune would be made. We went through a hundred names. Then I
thought of using a name we were emotionally involved with.
Gertrude, Fitz's mother's name, sounded too grand, and Victoria, my
mother's name, even more so. Tusia, an abbreviation of my mother's
name, was unpronounceable. Bet, Fitz's sister, sounded like gambling. Finally we agreed on Biba, after my sister. Biba's Postal
Boutique was born.

We tried the name out on Liz Dickson and Dimitri, then her husband. He said it sounded like a charlady's daughter, so we felt we had
got it right. We were not interested in high society but in real people
on the streets. We were both terribly excited. At last something was
happening.

The next step was a logo. During my days at Helen Jardine's I had
become very friendly with a fashion illustrator called Moira
McGregor. Her boyfriend, John McConnell, was a graphic designer.
We approached Mac who came up with an ace logo that looked like
a Post Office rubber stamp. We then found a receiving postal address
in Oxford Street.

Jill Butterfield featured our skirt one Monday in June 1963. The
picture was rather small but the address was there and so was a good
description of the skirt. Next morning we rushed to Oxford Street in

Fitz's sports car – hood down to accommodate the anticipated avalanche of mail. I sat in the car in Golden Square while he went to collect it. As he turned the corner on his return journey his face was very sad. In his hand he held a small parcel. We sat in the car and counted the letters. There were fifty envelopes with 2 guinea postal orders. After four days there were no more envelopes. We had totalled two hundred orders for skirts. The dress department at the Royal College sewed them and we packed and despatched them from our flat in Cromwell Road. We had made 6d profit on each skirt. This covered the daily petrol to Oxford Street.

There followed a denim children's dress in the *Observer* and another children's garment in the *Evening Standard*. We had no orders for these at all. Not one. It looked as if our new career had ended before it had begun. On the evenings after work, rather depressed, we had talked of taking one of those little advertisements on the back pages of newspapers. We invented the 'Wigechief', which was a cotton triangle scarf with a little false fringe sewn in the front of it. It was meant to cover your rollers as you did your housework. By then we were really scratching.

One Tuesday morning I had a telephone call from the *Daily Mirror*. Would I come up to Fleet Street and see Miss Felicity Green, the fashion editor – probably the most powerful of them all at that time. As her secretary showed me into her room I was terrified, but she really wasn't quite as frightening as I had imagined. Miss Green told me she was doing a feature on four career girls and she wanted me to be one of them. She had noticed Biba's Postal Boutique and wondered if I'd design and make up something for the feature. Nervously I said how about a pink gingham dress? She agreed, but felt it ought to have some interesting detail, so I suggested a hole in the back and a Brigitte Bardot kerchief to match. She said that sounded rather nice but it must be inexpensive. She felt 2 guineas was rather steep so I said, 'How about 30 shillings?' Miss Green said 25 shillings was nearer the mark. I said fine and went home.

Well, it wasn't fine. Fitz nearly did a back flip when he heard of my attempt at haggling. I have never dared to discuss prices again. Since that day my job has stayed at designer, to stop me doing everything for nothing! This division of labour has proved to be largely successful.

The sample was made up and looked really nice. The dress was sleeveless, had two darts and was quite short. The back had an enormous round hole in it. I had bought the sugar pink gingham in John Lewis, and had assumed that all the mills in Manchester were stacked with bales of sugar pink gingham. We sent the dress in to the *Mirror* and never gave it another thought.

On 3 May at 4 o'clock in the afternoon there was a call from Miss Green. Very sternly she said, 'Barbara, you do have a supply of pink gingham, don't you?'

'Yes, of course, Miss Green,' I said, shaking in my shoes. I relayed the message to Fitz, who immediately rang Humphrey, my mother's second husband, in Liverpool, and asked if he had any friends in the gingham business. Humphrey rang back and said he had met a friend at the golf course who said he had all the pink gingham we would ever need in a lifetime.

The following morning Fitz went to work as usual. He said he would buy the *Daily Mirror* on the way and ring me from the office. He was back home in five minutes clutching ten copies of the paper. The centrefold was divided into four unequal parts. The last was over three-quarters of a page. A great big beautiful picture of Paulene Stone purred sexily at us. She was draped in gingham checks – a smaller inset showing the detail of the big hole was positioned in the corner of the page. Miss Green's copy was short, sharp and commanding. We couldn't wait for the next morning. Fitz told me not to get too excited.

On 5 May 1964 very early in the morning we parked the car in Golden Square and waited for the hour when the first post would arrive. As usual I sat in the car while Fitz walked round the corner into Oxford Street. He took longer than usual. When he came back he had a grin from ear to ear and was dragging a huge sack behind him. I ran to help and didn't know whether to laugh or cry. We opened ten letters at random and they all had postal orders in them. We dragged the sack to the car and drove home. When we reached home we sat on the floor of the living room and tipped the sack upside down. We took bets on how many envelopes the sack held. Fitz won. It was four thousand letters. Later that day Fitz went back to work. I continued my drawings of the monstrous corsets for a newspaper advertisement. I had covered the letters with a blanket.

The next morning we thought we ought to go up to Oxford Street and see if there were any more straggling letters. As Fitz came round the corner he had a bigger grin on his face than the previous day. He was struggling with an even larger sack. As I leaped on him to hug him he said, 'Not yet, there's another sack left in the office.' That day the count was seven thousand letters.

We brought out all the casseroles, baking tins and saucepans we could find to use as sorting boxes – even the wastepaper baskets. Jenny Dingemans and Mary Potter came to help out. Every morning we collected more sacks. We now had £14,000 in postal orders and stamps of different value. To get to 25s with 6d postage and packing, there were dozens of permutations. Fitz gathered up the fortune into a paper bag and hand in hand we walked to Barclay's Bank in South Kensington. We felt like conquerors as we deposited the loot on the counter. The bank clerk looked up in horror as Fitz started unloading the bits of paper. He called another clerk over and they exchanged a few words and told us to 'push off' as it was only half an hour to closing time. We couldn't believe our ears. Here we were with £14,000 and it was too much trouble to count it.

'Right,' said Fitz, 'so you won't accept the money?' We packed up the postal orders, crossed the Brompton Road and went into the Midland Bank. The manager accepted us with open arms.

There were many more paper-bag deposits over the next few weeks. We had received seventeen thousand orders and all we needed now was 25,000 metres of sugar pink gingham. It was time to face the hard facts of making all those dresses. Our foremost worry was the pink gingham. Humphrey's friend sent down his salesman. The gingham that was supposed to last a lifetime turned out to be only 400 yards. But never fear, he said, he had all we wanted in a fractionally larger check.

The first manufacturer Fitz talked to said we would never get the dress made for less than £2 10s. Joanne Brogden again came to our rescue. She recommended a consultant, who in turn recommended us to Courtney Jones, a former world figure skating champion who was now a designer. He introduced us to Theo Savva, a Greek manufacturer, who welcomed Fitz with open arms and a bottle of retsina. He wanted to see the graded patterns immediately.

'What patterns?' asked Fitz. 'What's a graded pattern?' He telephoned me at home. Had I heard of grading? Yes, of course I had, but I had forgotten all about allowing for different sizes. Nick, Theo's brother, scratched his head. He had our order for ten thousand dresses, fabric was arriving next day, and he quite understandably asked for some cash in advance. Fitz's face fell; he had paid out all the money we had for the fabric.

The pink gingham dress is now a Greek legend. Theo always has a gingham dress hanging there for good luck. When the gingham fabric arrived Theo sent a cutting to Fitz at his office. He said, 'Mr Sime, this doesn't look like the picture.'

Fitz is partially colour blind so showed the cutting of gingham to his secretary. 'Is this pink?' he asked her. It was definitely not; it was bright scarlet and worst of all, the check was four times the size of the gingham in the photograph. For a final opinion Fitz sent the dreaded cutting in a taxi to me at Cromwell Road. I don't know if the taxi driver thought *he* was being taken for a ride, driving all the way from St Martin's Lane to Cromwell Road with a tatty scrap of checked fabric. When it arrived I thought it looked like a bistro tablecloth.

Luckily when we sent it back our money was refunded. I left the telephone off the hook in case Miss Green telephoned. But the next morning every mill in the North of England had heard that a lunatic was looking for thousands of metres of pink gingham. Our mail was full of swatches of coral, red, lilac, pastel pink and even pale blue gingham. Mr Rogers of Burgess Ledward got the order.

Fitz spent nights and days at Savva's while they sewed, drank, danced and ate Greek food. We had despatched seventeen thousand dresses from our flat in Cromwell Road and in each parcel was a note that said, 'You can now have a blue gingham dress.' We had another five thousand orders. Of the seventeen thousand dresses, only ninety were returned, which must be a record in mail order, and we had made a profit of 5s a dress.

Our next editorial write-up was with *Woman's Mirror*. It was a drawing of a brown pinstripe smock with the eternal matching kerchief. Fitz had priced it at two guineas. *Honey* magazine ran a double-page spread on a mix and match printed cotton blazer, skirt, trousers, Winnie-the-Pooh hat and blouse, and we were now a fully fledged mail order business.

Those sacks from Oxford Street were getting heavier and heavier each day. We needed to take premises to despatch the clothes from so we found a basement in Motcomb Street. It was so damp that my straight hair turned into a frizzy freakout in minutes. Fitz and Terry, a male nurse from a lunatic asylum, spent every evening packing. They managed to do two thousand boxes a night. Mary Archer Shee was our first full-time employee. She typed answers to enquiries and complaints, her hair growing curlier by the minute. Half an hour before the Post Office closed an armada would leave the basement of Motcomb Street. Mary Archer Shee would arrive followed by a funeral procession of taxis full of brown boxes. Terry and Fitz would be in the Post Office hurriedly licking stamps and sticking them on to the boxes. There never seemed to be any cash so Mary would haughtily offer the taxi drivers payment by cheque. After all this stamp-licking Fitz would go to the nearest pub with his tongue hanging out.

We got through by sheer brute force and ignorance. From the moment of that gingham dress we have been up and down but we have never looked back. Both of us still held our jobs during the day, but I found it very difficult to split my concentration between the drawing of all those awful clothes for other people and our own hilarious life in the evenings. Mind you, it didn't seem quite as hilarious at the time as it does now.

Our double-page spread in *Honey* attracted the attention of the Queen of the Mods, Cathy McGowan. The Friday-night television programme, *Ready, Steady, Go,* was becoming very important, although when Miss McGowan's secretary telephoned and made an appointment for me to go to the ITV studio I didn't know who she was until Fitz informed me.

I went to meet her at the studio in the Aldwich. As I was asked to wait in the lobby the lift door opened and a lovely leggy creature stepped out. She had long straight luminous hair with a fringe that hid her eyes. Her clothes were simple but immaculate. I thought it must be Miss McGowan's secretary. I was twenty-four and she only looked about eighteen. I was amazed how cosmopolitan her style was. Her taste was impeccable for someone so young. Cathy and I chattered and after that meeting we became great friends. She asked me to make her some clothes as she had liked the *Honey* feature. I was thrilled.

Apart from buying clothes from Kiki Byrne I had tried every dress-maker I could find, but very little worked for me, so I had to have clothes made specially for me. Being heavy-boned, as my mother called it, all I wanted was skinny-looking clothes. The French knew how to cut. I wanted clothes cut with armholes so high up the body that your torso looked long and skinny. Deeply inset shoulders and narrow sleeves made the silhouette even more angular.

I had always been fascinated by shops. I enjoyed pottering with objects and arranging them into patterns. In Jerusalem as a child I loved going into the local shop on the corner. Food was scarce but the couple who owned the shop took pride in displaying their cheeses on marble slabs with net umbrella-like covers and little blue beads round the base. Rows of sausages hung from a pole and on the floor there were sacks full of grain, beautifully laid out. I preferred playing shop to playing with dolls. Around now, in 1964, I suggested the idea of opening a shop to Fitz. He thought it was daft, as life would revolve around looking after it, but I was more and more infatu-ated with the idea of having a place to show the clothes off.

We had accumulated lots of rejects and garments that people had sent back to exchange for another. Without telling Fitz, I hauled them over from Motcomb Street to our flat and spent hours arrang-ing them round the living room, hanging them on door frames, fireplaces and cupboards in geometric shapes. The next day I tele-phoned friends and secretaries of press ladies to announce a sale. I put the record player on as loud as I could, playing a Beatles LP. By one o'clock our flat was seething. Every person I had telephoned had told at least ten others, who in turn had brought friends along. When I telephoned Fitz at his office to come and have a look, I had £500 in a shoe box I was using as a till. Our bedroom had been turned into a changing room. I even had trouble refusing to sell my cushions and casseroles. By the time Fitz arrived, the flat looked as if a bomb had hit it. He thought it was a fluke, but for days after, just as we were going to bed, somebody would arrive wanting to know if the sale was still on.

During junk hunting sprees, when I would drive around the side streets looking for undiscovered antique shops, I had spotted marvel-lous dilapidated corner premises in Abingdon Road in Kensington. It had been a chemist's shop and had been closed for quite a while but there were lots of black and gold signs left and the windows were painted halfway up with scratched black paint with gold leaf edges. The woodwork outside was covered in marvellous peeling blue-grey paint. I instantly fell in love with that place.

I dragged Fitz down there and he loved it too. We tramped up the road to the nearest pub to find out who owned it. They didn't know, so we visited other pubs and shops until we found someone who directed us to the basement where Mr O'Grady, the landlord, lived. We tried for days to contact him but he was never in. Then one Sunday morning we found him. Mr O'Grady said he wouldn't take less than £20 a week for the premises. We took it on the spot. In the evenings Fitz packed dresses and at weekends he painted the shop. We were both still working at our jobs.

I had just seen the film *Ivan the Terrible* and was knocked out by a Polish court scene where the floors were laid with black and white tiles, so we had to have those for the shop. Fitz painted the walls navy blue. We heard of a beautiful Dutch wardrobe, and when we went to see it, it cost £40. We hemmed and hawed as it was so expensive but we bought it – our first investment. We took off the low doors which were beautifully shaped, and nailed them at right angles into a table, which was going to be a cash desk. A friend lent us two bronze lamps with huge black shades. We made long curtains in a plum and navy William Morris print with a plum dress fabric lining. I refused to have the flaking woodwork outside repainted.

The following Monday we went to see Theo to persuade him to make us dresses of one style in a range of different fabrics. This was the famous smock with the very narrow sleeves. He said he would do it as a favour and we took him down to see our new empire. He said to Fitz, 'Mr Sime, you're mads.' The shop was miles away even from Kensington High Street, which was then a place where only old ladies shopped.

While our massive stock was being manufactured we had received two thousand orders by post for the chalkstripe brown smock with fluted sleeves and kerchief. Fitz was expecting a delivery of two hundred of these, all in one size. He thought he would use the shop for storing them, as the Motcomb Street basement was bulging with boxes. We delivered the dresses to the shop late one Friday night.

First thing in the morning Fitz dropped me there and drove back to Theo's to collect more dresses that were ready.

It was ten in the morning, the curtains were drawn across the windows. I left the front door open and popped into the loo. When I came out the shop was packed with girls trying on the same brown pinstripe dress in concentrated silence. Not one asked if there were any other styles or sizes.

I turned the record player on. I only had the one Beatles LP. The louder the music played the faster the girls moved and more people appeared in the shop. A silent queue formed in front of the cash desk. Each girl had a 2 guinea dress on her arm. Nobody knew the price, they just held their purses open. I had sold every dress by 11 o'clock.

As soon as I could get to the phone I called Fitz and said, 'Quick, grab any dress you can.' The shop was still full of people waiting for a delivery. When he arrived the car's hood was down and brown chalkstripe dresses were heaped up in a mountain behind him. Everyone left the shop and we sold in the street from the car. We were still selling that chalkstripe dress in one colour and one size six months later.

The morning my father left for the last time he was wearing a brown chalkstripe suit.

It took me a while to learn what impact the colours I had ordered would make when they were delivered from the factory. When I saw our opening stock it looked like a funeral. The blackish brown and dark prune looked awful. I could only save it by stitching gold braid on the necks and sleeves. Poor Mother was commandeered with her needle. Biba and she sewed braid all night. The dresses still looked awful to me but we opened the shop the next day.

We had been looking for a manageress and Liz Dickson suggested a girl called Sarah Plunkett who worked at Belinda Bellville's. We immediately loved her. She was so calm and dignified and ladylike. But was she too aristocratic for us? We took the chance and she turned out to be marvellous. Sarah could control a crowd without upsetting anybody.

After a couple of weeks Sarah could hardly stand up for exhaustion. She needed help. She pointed out that there were two little girls who came in every evening after work. They were so pretty, with long blonde hair, and couldn't she ask them if one of them wanted a job? An interview was arranged one evening after the shop closed. After we had flushed out the last customer, two beautiful blonde girls came in, Irene and Eleanor: Eleanor Powell, pure Saxon and a very formal Virgo; Irene, of Polish-Russian extraction – a dreamer with her head in the clouds. They looked like fresh little foals with long legs, bright faces and round dolly eyes. They worked in Harrod's export department, but they wanted to work at Biba. The only problem was we had only reckoned on one assistant. We felt we couldn't run to two, but the girls were adamant. No division. We took on the pair of them.

The combination of the three girls was great. Sarah was twenty and Irene and Elly sixteen. We were the first shop to stay open until 8 p.m. every night but even we had not realized how busy we would be after 6 o'clock. The girls became exhausted. While Irene and Elly's social life flourished by their being in the shop, Sarah's suffered. Her private life was outside the shop hours, and by the time she got home it was 9 p.m. Liz Dickson again came to our rescue. In the street one day she had met a friend who had been working in Capri. Liz Smith came for an interview, which was conducted outside on the corner of Abingdon Road. Now we had another glamorous twenty-year-old to take over whenever one of the others flaked out after a heavy day. They were a powerful band of lovely girls, and completely involved in the work.

Fitz and I now had no other life than Biba. When the shop opened we had both given up our jobs. Every morning we would feel great anxiety. We were never sure if our customers would come back again. One Tuesday morning the weather was awful. The sky was grey, there was a feel of a thunderstorm coming. The shop was empty. By noon the shop was still empty. I was feeling really depressed – it had all been a flash in the pan, the bonanza was over. We dashed up the road to Kensington High Street. It was empty, too. Not a soul, not one old lady with a shopping basket on two little wheels. We soon realized that the shopping public reacts identically to the weather and the political situation. When they are depressed, they are *all* depressed at the same time. When the sun comes out they are *all* happy and go out shopping. When the sun is hot they go to the park to sunbathe and you've lost them. When it rains, if you're a little shop they don't come, if you are a big store they stay with you all day. But it was this neurosis that we found so exciting. For Fitz it was like fishing, and for me it was like junking. You never knew when you would catch a big one.

Our Saturdays were always spectacular, whatever the weather. If it was raining the shop stank of wet wool and the floor would be awash. If it was sunny the groups of newly found friends would congregate outside the shop. It became a meeting place. Years later I had letters from people who met at Biba, spent their courtship in Biba on Saturdays, married, had babies and wrapped them in Biba purple nappies. Our neighbour called her dog Biba, and recently I heard a beautiful girl at the airport calling, 'Biba, Biba' to a little girl of six in a straw hat and smock. Her mother told me that she had named her after our shop. We had become a big part of many people's lives.

At twenty-six Fitz and I felt much older than the others, like Mum and Dad. We worried about the girls and their fast life. Some could cope, but many fell by the wayside by nineteen. The fashion for LSD terrified me. My real life had become a sort of trip so I couldn't see why others needed this dangerous stimulation. But I know when I was eighteen I used to take a Preludin in the mornings to feel I was jumping from the moment I opened my eyes, and I suppose it was the same. Sometimes I pinched one of my mother's purple hearts, which the doctor prescribed for her to lift her spirits when she was feeling low. It's quite funny to think how many middle-aged women in the sixties were unknowingly reliant on amphetamines.

I don't think our girls were promiscuous; they picked and chose. If they fancied someone they went right out and got what they were after instead of weaving webs and hypocritical traps, as we had to in the fifties. In their flats and bedsits they had no mother waiting for them to see if they came home with a crumpled dress. In the buoyant mid-sixties they all had jobs and they were not used to eating massive meals. They were the post-war babies who had been deprived of nourishing protein in childhood and grew up into beautiful skinny people. A designer's dream. It didn't take much for them to look outstanding. The simpler the better, the shorter the better. Their legs seemed to be never-ending. Suddenly London was filled with long-legged girls and boys who became envied all over the world.

The girls and boys started to travel on new all-in cheap holidays, and to pick up continental elegance, too. There were masses of them and they all seemed to flock to Abingdon Road. With Cathy McGowan endorsing our clothes by wearing them nearly every week on TV, there was a sort of underground grapevine which was growing daily. As soon as there was a new style the tom-toms would beat out a message throughout the clubs and offices and the shop would be full again. Every girl could buy a new dress for her evening date. They might all turn up wearing the same uncomfortable Biba smock that itched and stopped their arms from bending, but it was a uniform for an era.

The girls aped Cathy's long hair and eye-covering fringe. Soon their little white faces were growing heavier with stage make-up, lids weighed down with doll-like thick fake lashes. Their matchstick legs were encased in pale tights and low-cut patent pumps. Miniskirts led to the adoption of tights. They seldom needed to wear roll-ons or bras. Their bosoms and tummies were so tiny there was no need for the heavy upholstery. The natural form was beginning to show.

All classes mingled under the creaking roof of Mr O'Grady's wobbly house. There was no social distinction. Their common denominator was youth and rebellion against the establishment. Sarah was the red light for the beat offspring of aristocratic families, while Irene and Elly knew the young working girls. Stars and would-be stars also flocked to the shop. One night as we were closing a tiny blonde girl came in and began taking the clothes off the hatstands. Instead of trying them on behind the dangerously wobbly screens, she stripped off in the shop and proceeded to try on smocks and trouser suits. Fitz was told to stay in the back office as the tiny, uninhibited girl was prancing around dressed only in her knickers. She was magnetic – her skin was like marble and her features larger than life. It was Julie Christie, getting her wardrobe together for the film *Darling*.

One day a huge black limousine parked by the spiky railings outside the shop. A very strange group got out and sauntered in. All, female and male, were wearing the most exaggerated flared trousers. Ours were flared but not as much as these. For once I felt upstaged! The tops of those pants were so tight and so low on the hip they looked as if they might slip off. The boy who seemed to be the leader of the pack wore a sheepskin waistcoat. Excitement mounted in the shop. It was Sonny and Cher. Fitz and I had never heard of them. After their visit, during which they bought the entire shop out, Elly became very friendly with them and they visited her and she them for many years after. She would always send their daughter Chastity our newest baby clothes.

Another prominent American visitor was Richard Avedon. The young ones didn't know who the hell he was and I had to explain to them he was the top photographer in the world, and the one who had taken the pictures of Audrey Hepburn in *Funny Face*. This didn't impress our girls, who had their own heroes. These were Cilla Black, Sandie Shaw, the Beatles. Jane Ormsby Gore came to the shop wearing jeans she had cut off at the ankles and fringed at the hems. We were all ushered out from the back office to see this spectacle. It was odd at the time to see a society belle like this. She was tall and angular with short jet black hair and a striking, angular face. She and her boyfriend Michael Rainey had opened a clothes shop in Chelsea for male pop stars, called Hung On You. Sometimes Mick Jagger would come in with his girlfriend Chrissie, who was Jean Shrimpton's sister. As he waited for her he would sit on the table by the till, chatting to Fitz. So many famous people were seen in the shop that our girls became very blasé about it, though they would usually buzz us upstairs to tell us who was in. I could never resist the opportunity to have a peep at a star.

There was a lovely skinny girl who visited Abingdon Road very frequently. She was even thinner than the rest of the crowd. Her thoughtful face was really beautiful, with big grey eyes, a very high forehead and small, slightly turned-up nose. Her name was Lesley Hornby, and she became Twiggy. Our clothes were minute, but we were once asked by Justin de Villeneuve, her manager, to take them in. Fitz and I didn't really get to know Twiggy until, many years later, she and her husband Michael became our closest friends.

In early 1965 we acquired a new member of the family, Kim, who was barely sixteen. Liz Smith had left us to become fashion editor on *Petticoat* magazine, and later of the *Observer* Colour Magazine, a meteoric rise! I know Liz now says she was the only smiling assistant, but I was quite adamant that the girls should not impose themselves on the customers. We were not going to become another 'Can I help you, madam?' shop. I wanted the customers to feel at home, not hounded by sales assistants. More to the point, our customers would have fled if they had been accosted. Irene, Elly and Kim became their friends. There was one very serious little girl who used to come to the shop and scrutinize every garment with a beady eye. Fitz would watch her face to see what had made a reaction. If *she* ever bought anything it *had* to be good. At our next round-up for more staff, the girl with the deadpan expression had applied for a job, and Eva was with us right up to the end in Big Biba. All our girls wore Biba clothes at work and, later, to go dancing.

On Friday nights we would go to the TV studio to watch *Ready, Steady, Go*. Would Cathy wear a Biba dress or a Tuffin and Foale? Cathy was professional: she would wear the best clothes she had been shown that week. I was green with envy when she chose 'Tuffy Fluffies', as Fitz called them. Sometimes Cathy wore Laura dresses, imported by Top Gear in the Kings Road. Laura was a shop in the suburbs of Paris; the designer there was Sonia Rykiel. The shop I was most envious of was Top Gear. It was run by James Wedge and Pat Booth. They imported the most beautiful of the French clothes, the sort that appeared in *Elle*. John Stephen's Carnaby Street was growing from strength to strength. Tourists from all over Europe were pouring into London for cheap weekends. They could buy suitcases full of clothes for virtually nothing as the exchange rate was so good. London was vibrating with French, Italians, Germans and Swedes coming to listen to the music, see the shops and gawp at the beautiful girls. We were selling mounds of T-shirts, accessories and still those one-size smocks and Winnie-the-Pooh hats.

I had given up hope of getting the hats made outside because they were so difficult to sew. But one day a very strange lady came into the shop. She seemed very old to me, almost thirty, and she looked like a French existentialist. She wore violet stockings, black stiletto pointed shoes, a black and white dogtooth check pencil skirt and a ribbed skinny polo-neck jumper. On her Juliette Greco-like head she wore a black squashy felt hat. Round her beatnik legs hovered two pretty little blonde girls. That day Molly Parkin took over the manufacturing of our hat, which immediately became the Molly hat. Fitz was terrified of her because whenever Mol appeared she came to chase him for money. Our lookout would warn Fitz that

Molly was marching down Abingdon Road with her two little girls in tow. Fitz would leap out of the back window and speed towards the Earls Court Road to hide in the nearest pub.

In the sixties the girls were prepared to suffer to look good. Our long skinny sleeves were so tight that they hindered the circulation. We used most extraordinary fabrics. We discovered that our local big store, Ponting's in Kensington High Street, had a large fabric hall. It was a knock-down-price department store which bought up old stocks from bankrupt factories. Some rolls of fabric were so old that the edges were faded yellow cotton. We became very friendly with the fabric buyer, who would let us into the pitch-dark stockrooms to buy them. Not until we got the stuff back to Abingdon Road did we sometimes discover many more yellow stains when the fabric was unrolled.

Our big breakthrough was the first fashion T-shirt. I went to Admiral, the sportswear people, and asked them to elongate their classic rugger shirt. This became a dress when dyed in sludgy colours. We found some fuddy duddy firms who produced old ladies' underwear, and I adapted a vest with very high armholes and a skinny body. It had a little rayon ribbon running through the neckline. We then dyed it at least twenty different colours. At first our orders were quite modest, but for the opening of the season in the Big Biba they reached one hundred thousand. Fitz would call in some funny old reps and ask them to make a sample of their old lady shape in a Minnie Mouse size. You could see their faces thinking in disbelief, 'They're mad.' Then they would go away and after weeks of telephone calls and chasing they would come back with a sample. Two days after their delivery we would be reordering twice as many T-shirts. This would tickle them pink, but little did they know that in the future we would in many cases take over their whole production.

We recoloured football scarves, hats and socks in Auntie colours: mulberries, blueberries, rusts and plums. Sometimes there were disasters with dyes. The paint just washed out, as the printer had forgotten to give it the final bake that fixes the pigment to the fabric. People were walking round in faded grey op art print dresses. It never occurred to them to return them. A few irate mothers brought back dresses with faded geometric impressions. They got their 3 guineas back and stormed off vowing not to allow their daughters to cross our threshold again. To some mothers Biba represented 'filthy culture', what Auntie would have called 'vulgar'. Auntie and I were no longer on speaking terms.

We were becoming very cramped in our office out in the back of the shop. The changing facilities were uncomfortable, with only three screens offering any privacy. The shy ones would change behind the screens but the more uninhibited just stripped outside in full view of everybody. Sometimes they piled up their own clothes and the ones they were trying on into a heap on top of the screen, which sooner or later collapsed with a crash. Elly and Irene were forever picking up the broken lamps and tables. Fitz said we had to make the office-cum-stockroom into a changing room and try and rent the first floor from Mr O'Grady for an office.

We made a rough plan of cubicles for the changing room. When we moved out of the office word got out that it was already a changing room, and girls flocked in there to take all their clothes off. We propped up a few wonky mirrors against the wall and the first ever communal changing room was born.

Upstairs we took possession of a room for £10 a week. The word from Mr O'Grady was that on no account were we to use any more space, but we hijacked another room to store our deliveries of cloth to be made up into dresses. Our office had a huge hole in the floor. We took advantage and picked a hole through the beams into the ceiling of the shop below. We could see when the shop was full and help was needed. Tables were arranged so you wouldn't put your foot through the holes, but it soon became more dangerous than practical.

Janice Joseph, a friend's daughter from Cromwell Road, had joined us to reply to all the mail order enquiries. I was run off my feet between my workroom which was making patterns and clothes for Cilla Black and Cathy McGowan, looking after the growing business of accessories, and seeing endless reps who sold fabric. I had to see them all just in case there was something we could use. I needed help – an assistant to help me cope with everything. Sarah came to my aid. She had a young cousin who was a deb but who worked. Fitz and I were introduced to Rosie Markes on the corner of Abingdon

Road opposite the shop. We continued our interview on the bonnet of my Mini. The best people we ever employed were interviewed in the street just before the pubs opened.

Rosie's most precious possession was an apple green Cacharel skirt. If anything came into the shop that would look good with that skirt she would buy it. I was bugged. Cacharel's skirts and the famous crepon shirt that Emmanuelle Khan designed were fast becoming very covetable but their prices were fortunately out of reach for most of our customers. Cacharel's skirts sold for 8 guineas, and the crepon shirt was even more expensive.

The shop had the best music in town, selected by Elly and Irene. When we were slack, out came 'Leader of the Pack' by the Shangri-Las. The last LP of the day was 'Goodbye, Goodbye, We're Leaving You', by Peter Cooke and Dudley Moore, which was a sign to start tidying up.

The girls were becoming personalities in their own right. The London office of CBS made a film about a little country girl who comes to the big city and is transformed into a swinging sixties' dolly who ends up dancing in the Ad Lib. They used Elly as the girl for this success story, and the whole film was really about us. In America the film started off the legend of Biba. The English establishment rag trade came to see what the excitement was about. Theo could no longer cope with producing all our dresses by himself so his brother, who was manager of Alice Edwards' factory, would secretly make dresses for us at night when the directors had left.

Rosie and I battled with the sacks of poisoned pigeons that lined the curvy staircase up to the office. I think Mr O'Grady sold them to smart restaurants up the road. It never occurred to us to mend the hole in the floor, although it was becoming dangerous. The reps' faces were a picture as they were directed up the peeling stairway full of foul-smelling sacks to enter a room with a gigantic hole in the centre. The supposed desks were tables squeezed up against the wall so that the legs wouldn't sink in the opening in the floor. The chairs usually had only three legs.

We started selling jewellery by chance. Mr O'Grady, whose operations were wide and varied, was also a representative of Adrien Mann. He came upstairs one evening and showed me some lovely plastic beads in many colours. We took some and each evening he would deliver us more beads, bangles and earrings – anything that Adrien Mann was stuck with. We were too frightened to return them in case Mr O'Grady insisted we change our black and white check tiled floor for carpet flooring. Poor Mr O'Grady put up with shuffling feet for two years without a complaint. He said he missed us when eventually we moved out.

By summer 1965 we had outgrown Abingdon Road. The shop was so full on Saturdays that people couldn't move. We had noticed a grocer's shop in Kensington Church Street. It was empty and it had a large wooden front. Six months later it was still empty. We felt it was meant for us so we went to have a look inside. It was perfect but the agents said we had no hope of getting the lease. There were rich supermarket giants competing for it.

Fitz insisted on a meeting with the owner, Mr Jenkins, a grand old man who had been both MP for the area and a JP. As the representative for Chesterton's started to give Fitz a hard time, Mr Jenkins, who had been saying nothing but giving Fitz a strong stare, suddenly stopped the exchanges.

'That's all right,' he said to the agent, and then turned to Fitz. 'My hobby is phrenology, and you have one of the most interesting heads I have ever seen. You are bound to be a success – the store is yours.' Later, when we opened in Church Street, he came to see how we were getting on. He took one look at my head and said, 'I can't believe it, you have an incredible head as well.' On such lucky chances are lives made. . .

At Abingdon Road we had been without a name over the door for a year. I didn't like it when we put one up. It was like branding something. The shop looked much better without a name. If people wanted to find us they would. A designer called Julie Hodges had created some lovely wallpaper for Abingdon Road, so I asked her to do some more for Church Street. The premises didn't need any redesigning. The shop was beautiful in its natural state. One wall was full of mahogany shelves and the original counters were magnificent. Julie designed a blood-red wallpaper screen printed on photographic paper. We made velvet multicoloured cushions for the seats in the windows. The floor was going to be black and white check tiles as before.

Although the shopfront at Church Street was quite low there was still a large window area letting light into the shop. Somehow it lacked the mystery of Abingdon Road. Above it was an expanse of fascia waiting for a name to be put up. Julie knew a painter and fabric designer, Tony Little. He spent a lot of time up on a trestle painting the word 'Biba' in gold on a black background. On each window he painted a gold leaf circle surrounded by black Art Nouveau squiggles, and this became our logo.

The gold circles acted as a magnet on passers-by. People couldn't resist putting their noses up to the glass. 'Is it going to be a Chinese restaurant?' was a frequent enquiry. One of the workmen got so fed up that he stuck a minuscule piece of paper in the centre of the circle. It said 'Nosy bastard'. Everybody who lent forward to have a closer look at the little bit of paper would angrily jump back, often knocking the ladder on which Tony was balancing with his pot of gold paint. We had to remove the piece of paper to save him from serious injury.

As opening day approached I was getting more and more nervous. Maybe nobody would follow us the extra 500 yards up the road. We orchestrated a moving party from Abingdon Road to Church Street and arranged a photocall for the press. Our girls wheeled rails full of dresses all the way up Abingdon Road and down Kensington High Street to the new shop, followed by photographers. A pantechnicon arrived in Church Street full of hatstands and girls. The girls were holding Biba bags, in case the name of the shop didn't get mentioned in the stories.

I had been stationed in the new shop all alone waiting anxiously for guests to arrive, when it all happened at once. Cilla Black and Cathy McGowan arrived and so did a million other guests and gate-crashers. Cathy and Cilla clambered on to the lorry and helped to unload the hatstands, and the photographers had a field day. Music was thumping in the shop and the wine rapidly disappeared. Everybody had a good time.

When the last guest left it was 6 o'clock in the evening. The black and white *Ivan the Terrible* floor was awash with spilled wine – it looked *really* terrible and it took us two hours to mop up. We began to bring out the stock and fill the shelves with T-shirts for the official opening the following day. It was a long night. By morning my brain was still whirring but my body had gone to sleep, so we went and had a greasy breakfast at the neighbouring café. When we came back there was a queue outside the shop.

Chapter Six

My favourite moments were always just before a new shop was to open: the music would be turned on, the girls ready as if to go on stage, tension mounting and – bang – the doors would open and let in the first customers. This time the shop was full of people within moments. They examined everything – we had branched out into many new areas with everything dyed to match in a large spectrum of muted colours. There were big-brimmed hats, double-breasted wool coats, tights, gloves, bags, jumpers and shirts, dresses and underwear. Even the matching feather boas, which I had intended only to use as decoration, sold like hot cakes.

Our first Saturday in Church Street was astonishing. The shop was four times the size of Abingdon Road but as crowded as the little one had been. The pavement outside was milling with people, every window seat was occupied and I even saw our bank manager take a quick look inside. By the early afternoon the hatstands were bare but still more people came to look. Our worry now was how quickly we could replenish the empty stands. The changing rooms looked as if a bomb had hit them. At the end of the day, when the last customer went home, we were exhausted but happy. We got out the champagne to gather up enough energy to put the shop in order.

Every Saturday the takings were bigger than the previous week. There were moments when the shop looked as if locusts had attacked it. We always knew there would be another delivery coming but we were never sure which dress Theo was going to finish next. One Saturday the customers were sitting on the window seats and on the floors, waiting for a delivery. When it did arrive it was only a few blouses. Fitz and I were terrified of what would happen when this meagre lot was put out but every piece was sold and we just closed a bit early that day.

Two weeks after Church Street opened, in March 1966, a team of reporters from *Time* magazine arrived. The next day it was *Stern* and then *Paris Match*. In their usual unimpressed way our girls and the customers continued to crowd the shop. America and Europe had discovered, or invented, swinging London. Long before this the man in the street had taken exposed thighs as part of life, but all of a sudden there were wolf whistles and cries of 'Ooh, look at that one.' The more they exclaimed, the shorter the skirts became. Every week I thought that we surely couldn't shorten them any more, but magically there were a few odd inches to go. Tights and knickers became more colourful.

It was through absolute ignorance that the mini reached the streets. The short skirt was on the way but it was only seen in showrooms. Courrèges had made a strong impact on the world with his space age dresses. Mary Quant was the first British designer to show the mini but I still say that our dear old Theo Savva was the man responsible for putting the mini on the high street. When the jersey allocated for a little suit arrived at his factory it was steaming hot from the finishers. As Fitz bombarded Theo with telephone calls for more and more stock for the opening of the shop, Theo cut the somewhat stretchy double jersey without 'resting' it. Jersey that is not rested soon relaxes itself back to its proper width. It was not the uncut fabric that rested – it was the skirts! When I saw the delivery I nearly had a heart attack. The skirts were only 10 inches long. God, I thought, we'll go bust – we'll never be able to sell them. I couldn't sleep, but that little fluted skirt walked out on customers as fast as we could get it on to the hatstands.

Every visiting star seemed to come to Biba. Mia Farrow, who had just married Frank Sinatra, came in with Samantha Eggar. Sarah helped them choose dresses, bags, shoes and underwear. The next day she received a huge bouquet of flowers from Mrs Sinatra and later we received a letter from Frank Sinatra's secretary asking us to send all the colours of the cheesehole hat, which had amused him very much. The hat was felt cut with giant holes like an Emmental cheese.

John Lennon's new painter girlfriend Yoko had come to the shop to borrow a dress which Rosie helped her choose to use in her exhibition that night. Later, as we were watching the TV news, Yoko came on and cut up our smock into little pieces in front of a million viewers. Next day, Rosie was wondering if she still had a job.

When Barbara Streisand came in she was pregnant. The girls offered her a private room to change in but she refused, and joined the mob in the dressing room. She bought lots of smocks. Princess Anne came in with her lady-in-waiting. She had a smashing figure. No one dared approach her. Fiona von Thyssen was a regular when she visited London. Mick Jagger and Marianne Faithfull would come in, Marianne in a transparent blouse that shocked even our lot.

Our greatest thrill was when Brigitte Bardot came, just after her marriage to Gunter Sachs. They arrived one very busy Saturday. The shop was packed but as the news spread even more people rushed in. Brigitte wanted to try on some dresses but Mr Sachs would not let her undress in the communal changing room. Fitz and I and a friend were sitting in our airless office, an old stockroom. Suddenly Sarah came in and said someone wanted to change in the corridor. She had a big grin on her face and winked as she closed the door, so I had to peep and see who it was. As I climbed on a chair and looked through the chicken wire I couldn't believe my eyes. There was Brigitte prancing from mirror to mirror with just her knickers on and Gunter trying to cover her up. I said 'Fitz, you've got to see this.' Brigitte wanted to go out as she was, undressed, to get more things from the shop, and her husband was frantically trying to stop her.

One night someone broke into the shop, but not much damage was done. The following night our new driver, Stephen Bell, the son of an ambassador, volunteered to be a nightwatchman, mainly because he had nowhere to sleep. He had settled himself in a sleeping bag underneath the skylight. In the middle of the night our burglar came back, lowering himself down from the skylight and stepping on sleeping Stephen's head. Our brave nightwatchman fled, terrified, leaving the burglar in the shop. When we came in the next morning Stephen had locked himself in our office, where he had hidden from the intruder, shaking like a leaf.

Once Irene got locked in on a Saturday night. At closing time she was making up her face by one of the mirrors inside the shop and was forgotten. The following night a woman telephoned us at home from Northern Ireland to tell us that someone was locked in the shop. Biba's telephone was only for incoming calls and the woman had called to complain that she had not received a mail order dress, only to hear a grateful and tearful voice crying out for help. Irene had been locked in all night and all day. Another night Elly was in the loo when we locked up. She cried out for help for hours. When someone passed below she threw a spanner out of a window. The spanner landed on the person's head, so she was rescued and he had a sore bonce.

During that busy year, 1966, we opened a shop in Brighton. This brought us nothing but trouble. It was in a lovely Georgian house on the way down towards the sea from the station. We employed a manageress who lived above the shop, but we hadn't realized that she was a mobster's moll who entertained half the Brighton underworld! One day when Fitz and I went down we were introduced to characters like Carol the Arrow and Phil the Pill. Stock was disappearing by the armful, and when a very famous ex-boxer came to see the 'governor' in Church Street to demand protection money we felt we should call it a day. A Chinese shop assistant had been doing a roaring trade selling dope amongst the beads and bangles. After only ten months we closed the Brighton shop.

I was put off drugs at a very early age by reading *No Orchids for Miss Blandish* under the bedcovers at school. The drugs issue was worrying to us at the time because other boutiques were always being raided by the police. Staff often openly smoked pot in some shops. We couldn't bear the thought of being closed down after all we had put into building our business. So, ironically, we employed two stork-like boys in the shop as security guards. I thought they were very conscientious because they just stood there for hours with fixed gazes. Throughout the day they ate nothing but sugar lumps, which they kept in big paper bags among the cushions on the window seats. One day a friend remarked how funny it was to see these spaced out lads standing at the door. They had been completely out on LSD for weeks. We fired them. We were unaware of the fact that the biggest pushers in London were running a roaring trade from one of the window seats in the front of the shop.

One of our fourteen-year-old part-time Saturday girls told us hair-raising stories of sex and drugs in a household she often frequented. A very famous pop star had a harem of twelve-year-old girls living with him and the goings-on made my hair curl. Fitz thought he should tell her father, who occasionally did repair jobs in the shop. The man went off to have a look for himself; when he eventually came back he said, 'Cor, it was lovely, all them naked girls. I'm going back there again!' It was pointless to remonstrate with him.

We'd noticed in Abingdon Road that behind the screens there would always be a pile of clothes we didn't recognize. It was Sarah who said one day that 'customers' must be leaving their own clothes and walking out in the Biba ones without paying. It was difficult to imagine that someone could calmly walk out of that tiny, crowded shop and not feel guilty. After this discovery everyone that came into the shop looked shifty to me. Our signs were to the point. I argued with Fitz about this. It was like my matchbox of pennies under the bed. So we put up notices saying 'Thieves will be prosecuted'. We didn't use the euphemistic word 'shoplifters'; I think we were the first. I found it very unnerving but later got hardened. We always prosecuted. Later we gained a sort of ESP about them. When a girl was about to steal her eyes would dart from one assistant to another and she would generate a kind of shifty electricity. Some of our girls could spot them as they entered the door.

In Church Street we put in closed-circuit TV but it didn't work. Our lighting was so low that at times you could see someone putting something in her pocket but you couldn't see her head. By the time you rushed out to the front of the shop the figure had disappeared or you couldn't recognize her. Once in Church Street, at about 7 o'clock in the evening, I thought I would disguise myself and see what I could steal. I put on a sample frock and a nylon curly wig from my desk, smeared on scarlet lipstick and went into the shop holding a huge shopping bag. I went straight to the wigs on the counter, examined them, and slipped one into my bag. Then I proceeded to look at other things that were easy to lift. I didn't dare look at any of the girls, but I heard one say, 'It's a fella in drag!' So I *was* being watched! I felt quite nervous, but wanted to burst out with laughter.

Surreptitiously I filled my bag with clothes from the hatstands and I had the sensation that the girls were getting ready to pounce. I walked briskly to the front door. Three of them were at my heels. I was starting to feel quite panicky: should I reveal my identity now? I bolted round the corner into the street, screaming with laughter. Kim and Irene chased after me into the street, and I started yelling, 'It's me, it's me!'

'Come on, Kim,' shouted Irene. 'Let's get the bastard.'

I remembered the wig and tore it off. Their faces were a picture of disappointment when I turned round and they realized it was me.

Nutcases in the shop were common. One day a young girl came in stark naked except for a mini leather coat open at the front. She held a basket containing a large axe. She went up to the hatstands, gathered a few dresses into her arms and strolled down to the changing rooms, took a while choosing the dress she liked most, put it on, replaced her leather coat, picked up her basket and walked out of the shop. No one was brave enough to stop her.

We also had a few publicity seekers. One day a chauffeur-driven Rolls-Royce pulled up on the kerb outside the Church Street shop and a very well publicized buxom film star sauntered in, picked up an armful of dresses and walked straight out of the shop and into her Rolls-Royce. The car was still parked as two of the girls accosted the woman. Very willingly she came back into the shop with the dresses and was ushered into a little room to wait for the police to arrive. Usually the shoplifter would be in tears, promising to repent or adamantly stating that she had simply forgotten to pay. Not this one. She made herself at home and produced mirrors, make-up, combs and brushes out of her bag. While she was making herself up for the police, one of the girls became worried since this was clearly not a routine case. She went to ask Fitz whether we should actually call the police, since the woman could have stolen only for publicity. Fitz went to talk to her in the presence of two witnesses, as was the usual procedure. He said he wasn't going to call the police and kicked her out. She was very angry with him.

Once, to our regret, we caught the daughter of a very famous Member of Parliament. The media loved it. By the time the case came to court some days later, the judge accused us of encouraging her to steal. He said we knew what she was doing, and that there was a 'conspiracy of silence' on our part, as if we knew who the little darling's father was and were trying to make publicity out of it. It was sickening and absurd.

Sometimes shoplifters could be very nasty and vicious. Fitz had an alarm bell connected to the office put into the frame of the front door. It was an emergency measure and only to be used if it was really necessary. When it did go off in the office everyone left their desks to help – there would be Fitz, the dogs, and anyone else around. One day Elly chased a shoplifter up Church Street, catching up with her in front of the Carmelite Church. The shoplifter had refused to budge and lay down on the pavement. As Fitz and half the shop staff reached the spot, a wedding procession was coming out of the church and started lining up for photographs. Between the photographer and the wedding party was Elly, holding on to the shoplifter, with Fitz and another man like bookends on either side of the bridal couple. The wedding pictures must have been unusual!

After Biba had finally closed, people would tell us stories about a very famous English film star who used to boast about how much she was stealing from us. The laugh is on her. She was spotted very early on and all the girls were instructed to steer her towards the cheaper things. Once she had stolen something relatively minor she would go away happy for another two or three weeks. The effort of arresting her would have been out of proportion to the loss. Yes darling I do mean you.

However hard we tried, it was impossible to learn the rag trade's traditions and mysteries. We never envisaged there could be so many new problems: just as it seemed to be starting to make sense something awful would happen. We had a delivery of much needed smock dresses. We had been selling that style for ages so we assumed they were all right, but the sleeves looked odd – they were pointing backwards. It finally dawned on us that they had been put in back to front, and the smocks had to be returned.

A few weeks later, we had the delivery of our first trouser suit. We were determined to make really well-cut trousers, which were virtually unheard of then in England. We spent ages fitting away every crinkle and dimple from the crutch, but when they arrived from the factory they looked like harem pants, with great big wodges around the crutch. We were sitting in the shop after everyone had left, wondering what to do next, when a man walked in off the street. He started chatting and turned out to be a pattern cutter. Immediately I said, 'Please help us. Look at all these trousers.' He examined them and started laughing. He explained to us that all the backs had been sewn together and all the fronts were similarly matched. It was a relief to know what the problem was, but frustrating how often I was unable to solve a problem because of my own ignorance.

Towards the end of 1966 we moved into an enormous flat in Princes Gate, where we ran an illegal workroom for making samples. I had started to feel very tired. My head was aching and although everything was going so well, I felt depressed.

Fitz took me to Paris for a break. One evening we had dinner with Joe Dingemans, who had been the baby of the Dingemans family and was now studying at the Sorbonne. She took us to a fashionable bistro but I felt awful when the first course arrived. I took a few sips of soup and couldn't go on. As we left the restaurant I threw up. The next day we hurried home. I wondered if I was expecting, but we had been married for six years, so why should I get pregnant now? Eventually Fitz made me go and see a doctor. She examined me and confirmed that I was pregnant. I just sat there stunned. I never thought I would have a baby. The doctor, I could see, was worried by my reaction. She said, 'Doesn't your husband want a baby?' It dawned on me that she thought I had come to her to see if I could have an abortion. But of course Fitz wanted a baby – he would go wild with joy. When I left the surgery and got in the car, Fitz could see by my face what the news was. Even I felt better now that all that miserable feeling was explained.

It was time to start nesting. We found a lovely house a stone's throw away from the shop. It was to be our first real home. Julie Hodges printed a beautiful border for the nursery walls. Again we had our squiggly Art Nouveau paper in brown and gold. Rosie and I combed antique shops for furniture. Victoriana was still very cheap then and you could find marvellous tables, chairs, pictures and giant gilt mirrors for next to nothing. Brunswick Gardens was turning into an Aladdin's Cave.

At the same time we were talked into opening a winter shop in a hotel in Zermatt. We were going to ship over our black and gold paper, hatstands, lampshades and all the Biba knick-knacks. I was feeling better now, so Fitz and I went to Zermatt to see what we were getting into. It was late summer and after a very arduous journey by train up the mountains, which lasted a whole day, we arrived. We stayed on for a few days to supervise the photographic printed paper being put up and so on. Eventually we had had enough and we went home. Irene, Elly, Kim, Eva and the twins went to Zermatt in shifts to run the shop. They all had a marvellous time.

While I was still able to fly, Fitz and I decided to have our first holiday for years. It was March 1967, and we set off to Greece. It rained every day so we thought we would try Beirut, nearer the sun, and maybe we would go on to Jerusalem. I didn't know if I could cope with seeing it again. Being pregnant and in a highly emotional state, I cried and cried the first night we arrived in Beirut. We were staying in the St George's Hotel, on the edge of the sea where I had spent so many happy times with my father. Fitz decided we should not go on to Jerusalem. It rained continuously in Beirut for seven days, so we couldn't leave the hotel. We ate ourselves silly with delicious Arab food.

When we returned we moved into our new home. The last occupant had seemed quite eccentric but we didn't realize quite how. The house had, apparently, been a brothel and our telephone never stopped ringing. Our number was quickly changed but the callers at the front door continued for ages afterwards.

Fitz and I wanted lots of dogs and had always loved Great Danes, so Fitz found Othello, who was as black as coal, in a pet shop near Marble Arch. When he brought the puppy home he could hardly carry him up the stairs, Othello was so big. He had yellow slanting eyes, which is not supposed to be a very good thing for dogs, but we didn't mind. We already had a small black pug, Orpheus. Othello and Orpheus became friends, almost brothers. In the park they were an uncontrollable pair. Orpheus, more mature but only a quarter of Othello's puppy size, taught him lots of little doggy tricks. We laughed at their romps, but I'm sure they were terribly annoying to other people.

I was in the office right up to the day when the birth was to be induced. My mother, much more nervous than I, had come to stay with us. It was a relief to go to the hospital to get away from her lectures. On 19 June 1967 I went into the Lindon Wing in St Mary's Paddington. I didn't want to know about natural childbirth, which was very much in fashion even at that time. All I wanted was to have a huge whiff of gas and wake up and see a beautiful pink baby at my side. When I was shown my baby he wasn't pink and he looked like a stewed prune. I opened my eyes for a second, told Fitz it wasn't my baby, and passed out. Next morning, when the gas had worn off, my baby looked pink and plump and jolly. I was euphoric. What was all that nonsense about post-natal depression? I was delirious with happiness and so full of energy I thought I could float up to the ceiling.

From the moment I knew I was having a baby, I wanted him to have my father's name if it was a boy, but I didn't dare speak of this to Fitz. After breakfast, Matron came to my room and said that she hoped we had a name ready as the registrar was coming round. I telephoned Fitz in the office and blurted out nervously that I wanted him to be called Witold. Without any hesitation Fitz said yes, so the little chap was registered as Witold Vincent Hulanicki Fitz-Simon.

From an early age Witold spent a lot of time with us in the offices and the shop. He grew up with the girls around him. They were like his big sisters. Later we always advertised for nannies who were teachers, usually in transit from Australia or Canada, so that his life would be full of interest. They used to stay with us for a year or so.

After Witold was born I started designing children's clothes. There was nothing then for babies to wear except pink and blue stretch towelling suits, or those prissy looking woolly jumpers and bonnets. My baby was going to wear purple and black and other Auntie colours. In the winter he wore a brown Russian fur hat and jerkin.

We opened a children's department at the back of the shop, a dolls' house, just high enough for an adult to enter. We even cut down hatstands to fit into the house. None of the girls could stand working in there for more than two hours without coming up for air, but the children loved it. Biba babies started to appear in the streets with their mothers.

Much later, when we dropped the hem of our coats to the ground, we also made a maxi coat for the kiddies. Witold was the guinea pig. He was three years old and his blond hair was cut like Brian Jones of the Rolling Stones. His current nanny, Heidi, had an identical haircut. Unknown to us, instead of going to the park she would dress Witold and herself up in the latest clothes and parade up and down the King's Road. One night we were watching the late night news on the television. I was half dozing when Fitz shot out of bed. 'Wake up, look at this!' Witold and Heidi had been stopped in the Kings Road and were being interviewed. Witold was expounding on the maxi coat: he quite liked it, but it was awful to play in!

*

Mother, now living in Hove, was a perfectionist. She liked to see every room immaculate, every cushion puffed up. The ashtrays would always have to be sparkling clean and when with us she would rush around with a duster skimming away imaginary grime. I am untidy for long spells but after a while, when things get out of control, I have bursts of obsessive housework. When our home became so cluttered with statues and objects collected in junk shops that you couldn't move without breaking something, I found a novel way of dusting – with my hairdryer. The dust would just float up into the air and land on something else but you could, if you were very nimble, redirect the dust with another blast from the dryer to a more convenient spot, such as a sofa. You could then remove the layer with a Hoover. The process was laborious but it didn't feel like housework, it was much more industrial. There were no domestic sacrifices on my part.

When we married, Fitz and I made a pact that we would look after our own clothes. Witold was brought up in the same routine. As we were growing richer, instead of buying a washing machine, which I could never understand how to use, we would buy a new shirt and pair of socks a day. Fitz was the proud owner of 120 white shirts and socks worn only once and then thrown into a cupboard. The laundry bill after 120 days was astronomical. By then I was a fully fledged domestic slut.

When the neurosis of wanting possessions disappears there is very little incentive to buy things. If you can look in a shop and know you can afford to buy all the things you want, you have no desire to possess them. I had reached the stage where I had everything I had ever wanted – there was no more room to place another antique. My wardrobes were bulging with clothes that I only wore once. My fridge was always empty because we usually ate out. My dressing table was groaning with expensive scents and antique jewellery hung as in a casbah. When an Italian gossip magazine came and did an article on me at home I suddenly saw myself in a new light. The photographs were very beautiful, but I was revolted by the jackdaw nature they exhibited. Bloated with possessions I could never hope to use or enjoy, I felt I should rid myself of these trappings.

Orpheus died and Othello was desolate and moping, so we decided to get another Great Dane puppy. We found a kennels that bred blue

Great Danes. As Hannibal grew bigger his colour became more and more blue, as if he had a mist surrounding his body. He was frail, and never stood a chance against the butch Othello. The dogs usually came to work with us, and there were many reps who were too frightened to enter the reception area. Others got used to the sight of contented dogs lying on leopard skins, chewing on the carcass of a cow and occasionally growling playfully at each other.

Othello was definitely boss of the two dogs. When they were romping around playing and growling it sounded as if they were about to kill each other. Othello would always attack poor Hannibal's balls when at last they dropped. One day he went too far and bit them. The only way we could stop Hannibal licking them better at night was to make a grey satin ball bag which looked like two massive pouches attached to an elasticated G-string. During the day I would hang his ball bag on the doorknob in our bedroom. Once my mother came to stay with us. We were watching television with her in our bedroom when I suddenly saw her gaze gripped by the contraption hanging on the doorknob. I decided not even to try to explain.

At times, when the dogs wanted a bit of love from Fitz, they would sit for hours like statues on a pair of high-backed ornate chairs placed on either side of his desk. If ever Fitz had anyone in his room who might be sitting on 'their' chairs they would just pad into the room and put their great big heads under the poor unfortunate visitor's backside and turf him off. We didn't notice how ill-mannered they were.

As the dogs grew older and bigger, their unruliness became a major problem. They were as good as gold indoors but as soon as they hit the street there was chaos, so we sent for the world's leading expert – Barbara Woodhouse. She arrived armed with two unbreakable leads and an LP on how to train animals. Othello was led to the mews at the back of the shop, pulling as usual, Fitz heaving away in the rear. Mrs Woodhouse strode forward and seized hold of the lead. Othello sat on his haunches, dug in his front paws and refused to budge. We explained that this was not usually the problem. Mrs Woodhouse heaved and shouted commands. Othello gritted his teeth and bulged his neck muscles. Mrs Woodhouse bulged her neck muscles. A crowd from the local pub filled the end of the mews and started cheering from both sides. Fitz started taking bets on Othello.

Mrs Woodhouse retired and Othello, once we had hold of him again, rushed up the mews, scattered the crowd and broke one of the unbreakable leads. It was a KO victory for Othello.

I had got through the depressing bits of my life before by slipping into fantasy and dream. When I met Fitz he made my fantasies come true. Biba was like a fantasy. I didn't like the way I looked, but the classic Biba dolly had all the attributes I lacked. She was very pretty and young. She had an upturned nose, rosy cheeks, and a skinny body with long asparagus legs and tiny feet. She was square-shouldered and quite flat-chested. Her head was perched on a long, swanlike neck. Her face was a perfect oval, her lids were heavy with long, spiky lashes. She looked sweet but was as hard as nails. She did what she felt like at that moment and had no mum to influence her judgement.

As time went by my Biba girl became more dreamy and untouchable. Her long straight hair turned into a halo of golden ringlets, her cheeks were hollowed by brown powder, and her lips stained with sepia lipstick. The thin line of her brows framed her sparkly blue eyes. Once she had formed into a person it was easy to think up dresses and all the other things that she might want to use. She was so young and fresh that all those Auntie colours that I had hated when I was young looked new on her. In the daylight the orchids, dusty blues, bilberries and mulberries looked quite in tune with her surroundings. Once she was inside Biba, the music thundered, the lighting was soft, and she became more mysterious. It was extraordinary to see how people applied, often successfully, my dream image to themselves. I felt we gave them basics that they could then interpret in their own way. I could sit in the shop for hours watching customers who had previously bought things and now were wearing them with a completely new slant.

If one season bags were big sellers it didn't mean this would continue. By next season everyone had a bag and wanted shoes or belts. The steady sellers were always mini dresses and T-shirts. Fitz was forever nagging me for more dresses and coats. We would never run a winner dress too long, to keep stock in the shop looking fresh, but we'd make another style very like it. The exception was a rubberized mac that was our best seller for six years. We would just alter the length to whatever the mood of the moment was.

We learned not to exceed the limitations of a manufacturer. It was very important to know what he was capable of, so that I could do designs that fitted into his production method. One of our problems had been someone to fit the samples on. A clothes dummy wouldn't do because they have no arms or legs. If you fitted on someone who was a fraction imperfect somewhere, this fault would be magnified ten times in production. We finally found the most perfectly proportioned 'dummy' body – it belonged to Delicia Howard, a part-timer in the shop. She told me, 'I spent years getting a degree and then I got a job because of my body and not my brain!' Del's brain was something, too, so I hijacked her over to the office. For the next eight years her domain was cosmetics and household, but during all those years she continued to do fittings. She carried on with her job, telephone pressed to her ear, while somebody stuck pins into her. Never once did I hear her grumble about having to strip throughout the day to try on yet another sample.

Eva was also recruited from the shop. One evening I was sitting in the window seat wondering how the hell I was going to muster up energy to display a mass of trousers lying in a heap on a table. I saw Eva go over to the table and very methodically fold them and arrange the colours in a most beautiful way. She really understood clothes. Eva was put in charge of accessories.

Rosie had left to start a business, so Elly introduced me to a flatmate, Daphne, who was a fabric designer. She took over the job of cloth research. With her knowledge of printing we were now able to buy in prints and have them coloured up to our own specifications. Daphne's job was to look at every fabric all over Europe. The originals of specialist items like hats, shoes, bags and belts were always viewed in the factories. I would do the sketches that they worked from. Those years of fashion drawing now came in very useful. We went to Italy for bags. Sometimes they were made from my drawings, or if there was anything interesting we would adapt it to our needs. The same thing happened with knitwear: basic shapes were made to our specifications in special colours in Hong Kong, but for the extra-special knits we would visit Italian fairs. There would always be an exciting yarn that we ordered in our shapes and colours.

Most stores would send five or six buyers for a week for the work we did in a couple of days. Doors began to open to us as we became known. We went to great pains to find good manufacturers. In Paris we went round the shops surreptitiously ripping out labels that gave away the name of the supplier. If I went into a store in any part of Europe and saw something I liked I felt I had failed if I didn't know where it was made.

The glossy establishment press never took us seriously. We were just a gimmick. The fact that we sold to real people and not just jet-setters made them ignore us. The popular press, however, seemed to love us. To me success was not a photograph of an unwearable, over-priced garment in a glossy magazine. My personal measure of success was when I had a street winner on my hands. People bought it and that meant they liked it and that was my reward. Even if the garment was a good design, something that didn't sell took on a sad look. A winner seemed to have a halo round it. In the sixties glossy magazine fashion editors lived in cloud-cuckoo-land, still dictating to a minority. They had forgotten that their function was to report and edit for the public, not to instigate. *Queen* in the early sixties was very influential but too toffee-nosed. *Elle* was the first young magazine, and at the other end of the scale *Rave* was the voice of the pop world.

Among the establishment rag trade there seemed to be a theory that in order to sell, clothes had to be bland and badly designed. I couldn't see why you had to patronize the public – they weren't stupid. I wanted everything Biba sold to be beautiful, and it worked. Designers at that period seemed to feel they should dictate to women. I couldn't see how they knew what women wanted – those designers were usually men. The young wanted to be led but not dic-tated to. It is fatal to be too far ahead just for the sake of being able to say that you were the first. It is much more difficult to be just one small step in front of the public. It's useless to present them with clothes they don't yet understand. You have to respect street wisdom and nous. I was deliberately rather unaware of what other people were doing at this time because I found it discouraging to look too carefully. If they seemed to be doing much more exciting and inter-esting things than we were it would completely throw me.

It's easy to make a beautiful one-off sample but it's another thing to get it made in large numbers. A machine cannot imitate the magic a human being can inject into a dress. You can make a sample in the workroom that is simple and has soul. When it comes back to you from a manufacturer it may seem identical but lack any feeling. I would pat and talk to rails of dresses to put some life into them. It was amazing what a difference this made. Even a driver can make a difference when he loads up a van. If he treats the clothes with respect they seem to come to life. Some manufacturers have that magic. You can tell when they really care, and those deliveries would always sell out first. There I was patting my rails of dresses and telling them they could be lovely if they tried; Fitz was doing the same but his words were more direct: 'Go on, you bastards, go out there and sell!' There were always a few last dresses that wouldn't sell, and they needed a kind word to cheer them up.

Cloth suppliers tended to dye only royal blue, beige and an awful dull red from year to year. Even black was difficult to get. Biba was definitely worrying the trade, showing them a market that they didn't even know existed. One large company copied every dress we put in the shop. Other rag traders spent a fortune buying their samples from us, but the cheekiest one, a well-known lady proprietor of a big dress company, would insist on returning the dresses after she had copied them and demanding her money back. How mean could you get? Other manufacturers would follow our vans around to find out where our things were being made so that they could copy our patterns.

Our personal life revolved around the shop and Witold. We rarely went out and when we did it was with the Biba girls. At night we were far too tired to do much. It's strange how your happiest moments seem very monotonous at the time. If we did go to a party, people invariably moaned, complained and were rude about the shop.

I didn't like my brothers-in-law so I scarcely saw my sisters. My youngest sister, Biba, came to work in Church Street, but not for long – she was so rude to everybody. She felt it was immoral to work so hard, and for money. Biba's husband, Bill, thought we should pay her a percentage for using her name. This made Fitz furious. Our relations were very strained.

One afternoon workmen had arrived and started to drill holes in the shop floor for the staircase. We were going to move the changing room down into the basement. We had stacked up the clothes on to rails and moved all the hatstands into one corner. I had taken everything off the counter to rearrange it, and I was standing there thinking how I was going to make the shop look different by moving the stock around. The drills were making an awful lot of dust. Fitz came through from the office. He said that Felicity Green had just telephoned. She was bringing Hélène Lazareff, editor of *Elle*, to see the shop. My heart sank. Why do such important things always happen to you when your knickers are down? We had half an hour to get the shop looking right. By the time they arrived the shop was looking immaculate and the workmen had been sent packing. Outwardly composed, but nervous, we waited. Hélène Lazareff was knocked out – there is something magical about being alone in an empty shop. The music was playing and the two ladies flitted around.

The next week *Elle* sent in their fashion editor, Claude Brouet, and they photographed many of the clothes. A few months later *Elle* published eight beautifully photographed colour pages of the shop. The headline was 'Alibiba'. They had used our girls as models.

Julie Hodges transformed the new changing room into a bordello. The walls were scarlet and the carpet an even deeper red. I searched for giant gilt-framed mirrors which today cost a fortune, but then I paid no more than £30 each. My collection of china pedestal jardinières was growing. Unfortunately they had a very high mortality rate in the shop. We never paid more than £5 for them, because they were still unfashionable then.

After a year the house behind the Church Street shop was bursting at the seams. The top floor was allocated to pattern cutting and sewing the first samples; the ground floor was occupied by the receptionist, the dogs, reps, Fitz's office, and a little hole of a room where Rosie and I sat with samples of dresses to go into production, and prototypes of all sorts of accessories, swatches of fabric, shoes, scarves, knickers, bras and hats. We needed more space. Conveniently, we found more spacious premises across the road, and the shop offices moved in there. The mail order part of the business was to take up the little house.

Each day we had dozens of letters from people who wanted to buy from us by post, and we were looking for a way of expanding. Mail order seemed a natural way to go. It was where we had started, and there was no doubt that the potential customers existed. I couldn't wait to do our first catalogue. For the first time I could actually realize on paper what the perfect Biba dolly should look like. The catalogues had to be much more professional than our own homegrown graphics, and we needed a new logo as the squiggles round the circle were looking a bit tired. John McConnell, who had designed our original mail order logo, came up with another ace, which we kept until the Big Biba. He also thought of the long narrow shape for the catalogue, so it would not be damaged when it was squeezed through a letterbox.

I could now work, through the catalogue, with top photographers whom I had always admired. My first choice was Donald Silverstein. I found it a great strain working with very strong professional people, as there was always a danger that they would take the situation over and it would become their vision and not Biba. Neither could I cope with controlling top models, who are usually terrifying. There were many perfect Biba girls in our own shop, but they were not necessarily photogenic. One outstanding girl looked like a miniature Jean Shrimpton, as skinny as a beanpole with a lovely little head. Her name was Maddy Smith. Maddy got the first catalogue job.

The second and third catalogues were photographed by Hans Feurer and the girl we chose this time was Stephanie Farrow. The fact that she was Mia Farrow's younger sister influenced me, though Stephanie did also have the most angelic face. By the fourth catalogue I had enough courage to approach one of the greatest photographers of all, Helmut Newton, who became famous for his books some years later. When it was time to photograph the fifth catalogue, Molly Parkin, then a fashion editor on *Harpers and Queen*, recommended a new photographer called Sarah Moon. Sarah's photos were stunning, very soft and feminine. Our last catalogue was done by Harry Peccanotti, but it was Sarah to whom I went back for all our Biba posters. She understood completely what Biba should be and was. Her work for us was some of the best she had ever done. Much later, in the Big Biba at Derry and Toms, one of my favourite photographers was James Wedge, who used to own Top Gear in the Kings Road.

In the summer of 1968 we brought out our first catalogue. We took some advertisements in *Honey*, *19*, and the then very influential *Petticoat*. The response was immense. Over a hundred thousand girls wrote asking for the catalogue. The cost of printing and postage in those days was minute. It cost us no more than 1s 3d to print and mail each catalogue. Our prices were still incredibly good value. Dresses were around £3, blouses £2, and very few things – even coats – cost more than £8. We'd forgotten to put the prices into the first edition of the catalogue, but this did not deter the punters who seemed to know the clothes would be good value.

But now for the first time in our lives we had to employ bureaucrats. We hired a manager and he hired an assistant manager. We had a 5000-square-foot warehouse in Chiswick, quality controllers and packers, and more managers. Each manager was trying to expand his own little empire. Each one had to be consulted and cosseted. Each one loathed the others. Fitz was going crazy trying to keep things running properly.

Although we knew more or less how much income each catalogue was going to generate, we found it impossible to forecast the sales of any individual garment. One of the photographs showed an outfit of a skirt, a jerkin, a hat and a blouse. For good measure Hannibal, one of our Great Danes, was sitting beside the model. That blouse alone sold fourteen thousand, and the other things sold about three thousand between them. The result was a shambles. We had to find 28,000 yards of fabric overnight, and we had to find the extra manufacturing capacity to make fourteen thousand blouses in about two weeks.

We discovered that our customers would happily wait about fourteen days for their delivery. After that they started to write to us asking what was happening. This was all right if their order was on the way, or going off in a few days. If not, we had to reply to them. In the case of the blouse, which was fairly typical, nearly all fourteen thousand customers wrote to us in the third week, and as the blouse was still at least two more weeks from being delivered, we had to reply to each one. For this we needed still more clerks and more managers to deal with the complaints. It was a nightmare. We had about fifty people answering letters to fourteen thousand other people all because one blouse had been too successful.

The huge administration needed to run this type of business was out of all proportion to the return. We had either to put up our prices to a level that would be unacceptable, or to forecast exactly the sales of each garment. Fitz spoke to several experts from the big mail order firms and discovered that even they really had no idea of how much any one thing was going to sell before they started to get a reaction from their customers. So Biba mail order was phased out, although it had been such a success.

Up till 1969 we took only cash and no cheques. We had been taken for a sucker by a notorious man-about-town who bounced a cheque for 3 guineas on us. We felt he didn't have much style! We were taking around £10,000 a week in Church Street. Multiply that by five to get the correct value today. Every penny went back into the business to buy more cloth to keep those hatstands full.

The Cyril Lord Carpet Company collapsed and one of their warehouse-cum-shops was empty in Kensington High Street. It was nine times the size of our Church Street shop. The ground floor alone was 3000 square feet, with another 1000 square feet of mezzanine, but the big attraction was the basement: a beautiful open area of 5000 square feet. To buy it was a huge undertaking, in terms of both organization and expense, but we felt we had to keep moving forward.

In order to help finance the move, Fitz decided to do one last catalogue. Everything that could go wrong went wrong. The response was slightly smaller than we had expected because we did the mailing when the summer buying season was almost over. Fabric suppliers let us down; one of the big winners was cut badly by a factory and had to be scrapped. Almost overnight we were transformed from a booming, growing business into a financial disaster. Biba at that time was not a limited company – if we had made it one we would never have been given the credit by our suppliers that we needed to finance our ever-growing sales, so Fitz was what was known as a sole trader and all the debts were his personal responsibility. Our suppliers, many of whom hadn't been paid for months, were demanding their money. To raise some cash to pay the wages and keep the shopfitting going, we had a giant sale at Church Street.

We saw that we had to look for outside investors, but no one would invest in a huge, half-decorated shop that had yet to take a penny. We simply had to open the shop and prove that it was a viable proposition. A close friend, Peter Church, and his gang of carpenters and decorators were literally working 24-hour shifts. Fitz and I helped them at night, and in the daytime Fitz would disappear to the City, where he was trying to persuade someone, anyone, to provide the finance.

The last four years had been very fast, but I wasn't prepared for this new drama. I had believed that hard work always brought rewards of security, but now it was obvious that it didn't. Every time I went into the shop I was afraid it would be for the last time. We found that the worse things became, the more we would need to smile. When you're in real trouble you seem to get most publicity. It can be very trying to sit through interviews forcing yourself to sound and look positive. Once somebody sensed any uncertainty on our part, the mood would spread. Although the staff seemed unaware of how grave the situation was, the vultures were circling above us and the reps had smelled blood. They surrounded the reception desk, not unreasonably waiting for their money.

I had confidence that Fitz would come up with something. He could always solve the worst of problems. He would just go to his office, close the door and sit and think, and find an answer or the beginning of an answer. Finally he made contact with Robin Napier, a director of the huge financial house of Charterhouse Japhet, and a Biba fan. Strange accountants appeared and started going through our books to verify the story Fitz had told. Robin Napier organized a consortium of his company, Dennis Day Ltd, a big garment manufacturer whose boss, Wally Rose, had been a tower of strength to us, and Dorothy Perkins, the big fashion retailers, whose founders Alan Farmer and his son Ian were still in control.

Between them the bank, Dennis Day and Dorothy Perkins were to own 75 per cent of Biba. Fitz and I would be left with the remainder. Fitz was to be Managing Director and I was to have complete creative control, and, most important of all, Biba would be properly financed at last.

Even with everyone finally agreed on the deal, the legal ramifications were horrendous. At the final meeting, with over twenty people around the table, bankers, directors and platoons of lawyers, there was a hitch and it looked as if everything had fallen through. It seemed as if the meeting were going to break up as the advice of tax counsel was needed. The room fell silent, everyone looking at us. Fitz looked at them all and said very quietly, 'If we don't sign today, we're finished. I can't hold out any longer.' Robin Napier asked us to leave the room. We were shown to somebody's office. We said nothing to each other, just waited, both of us saying our prayers.

The door opened and we were called back into the meeting. Everyone was smiling and shaking our hands. Contracts were signed and champagne appeared. Manny Davies, a great character and partner of Wally Rose, with a cigar permanently fixed in the corner of his mouth, came over to Fitz and said, 'This, boy, is your lucky day – I never thought you'd do it,' and he patted him on the back.

Chapter Seven

Each one of our new partners seemed to have done the deal with us for different reasons. Wally Rose of Dennis Day (dress manufacturers whose slogan was 'Dignity, Design and Distinction') thought that he would sell millions of Biba dresses to his customers through the big mail order catalogue. He could also see a dazzling future in supplying the three hundred or so Dorothy Perkins shops with our things. The Farmers and David Roxburgh, then financial director of Dorothy Perkins, wanted to add a bit of glitter to a rather old-fashioned image. Charterhouse Japhet genuinely felt that it would be a disgrace if Biba was allowed to collapse. They also felt that there could be disastrous repercussions for the rag trade as a whole, for if we went down financial confidence in everybody in the field would be shattered.

We had met Wally years before. Cathy McGowan had launched a section inside one of the Great Universal Stores mail order catalogues with him and she asked us to make up the prototypes of the dresses for her. Wally had proudly shown me every dress on the rails. I'd kept giggling because in my eyes they were frumpy Auntie dresses, until he turned to me and said, 'Barbara, you love your Biba but I love these dresses here just as much.' He made me feel an absolute heel. I never did that again.

Although both our new partners were public companies, they were run by their founders, who, like us, had had their ups and downs and were passionate about their own businesses. Wally and the Farmers could understand, without necessarily agreeing, why I fought for points that would strengthen Biba's growing image. Biba was only a baby and had to be protected. Alan Farmer and his son Ian could understand why we didn't want Biba clothes in Dorothy Perkins shops. The two signatures were like chalk and cheese. Dorothy Perkins in those days still had the knicker and bra image that they had started with over fifty years before. It was only later, when Biba was strong enough, that Fitz felt it was right to distribute the cosmetics through Dorothy Perkins.

Fitz and I were very fond of the Farmers. It was touching to see the way Alan Farmer spent most of his retirement travelling round the country in his Rolls-Royce visiting the manageresses of his shops. One day Alan Farmer came into the Kensington High Street shop and saw one of our girls in bare feet. He complained to Fitz, who replied, 'Bare feet maybe, but she has just taken a thousand pounds.' Alan Farmer never again interfered in the way the girls looked.

One day visiting Bracknell, the Dorothy Perkins headquarters, I found they were modernizing the offices. I couldn't understand how they could get rid of all that beautiful custom-made 1930s' furniture. I begged Alan Farmer to let me have the pieces in his office: a giant walnut desk, a miniature of it for his assistant, a cocktail cabinet with walnut shelving, and a small boardroom table and chairs to match. He was amused by the request and thought I was a little mad, but he had the furniture sent round the next day.

The thumping, thundering music caused some rumpuses, but the more complaints we received, the more I was convinced we were right. But complaints about the clothes were hard to stomach. We were told that our clothes fell apart! We knew that our quality was good, if not better, than anybody's. There are still many Biba dresses in people's attics. A certain type of person, however, associates quality with price, and since we were offering the best value anyone could find they were convinced the goods must be shoddy. We were producing at a manufacturer's price, cutting out the entire wholesale profit and taking the minimum mark-up possible. We always offered about 30 per cent better value than any other shop.

I realized now that up to the time of the crisis I had only been giving half of myself to the business; the other half I had held back. One morning I woke up and decided to take the plunge. From now on all of me would go into this business monster. It had to be all or nothing. It wasn't ambition, it was a desire to learn and see how large it would grow. The baby Biba was insatiable. Whenever I had slackened off I would pay for it the next day – there was no moment to relax.

The girls picked up the atmosphere of urgency and became equally absorbed. They gave their all during the day but at night they could cut off. Fitz and I went home and lived it for the rest of the evening and took it out on each other. We lived and thought Biba. The more energy we put in, the more we got in return from all who worked for us. There were no passengers, and there were no scapegoats. If something was wrong it was Fitz's or my fault for not spotting it and we didn't take it out on our employees.

Though we were in business to make money, we wanted to take it by merit and not by deception. We were interested in how cheaply we could sell something, not in how much we could get for it. The welcome mat in the new shop *meant* 'Welcome'. It was not some phoney trick to make people buy more.

We worked for months to get the new shop ready. Unlike Church Street, where we were still trading, it was a modernized shell. The pillars had been boarded over but we knew there must be something good underneath the blockboard. We discovered twenties' Egyptian-topped columns. This time I wanted to try to get away from the boudoir feel. The ground floor was going to be light and airy with marble floors. We both agreed the whole front should look like one big entrance to a store, but we would stick with our formula of shelving units that looked like giant dressers.

Julie Hodges had formed a shopfitting and decorating company with an architect and a businessman. We used them to do the detailed drawings and some of the actual work on the shop. Peter Church and our own carpenters would do the woodwork. We learned that St Paul's School, down the road, was about to be demolished. It was full of beautiful carved wood panelling pillars and stained glass windows that were to be auctioned. We put in a bid of £100 and got a huge bounty of panelling and stained glass. Reassembled, the wood became the gallery, a mezzanine which had been a boxed-in office. The boarded-over stairs to the basement revealed a handsome stair rail. The place was beginning to take on a strong feeling.

The architect, who was also to supervise the work on site, got off to a bad start when the very first hole he made in a wall was in the wrong place. What was left was a narrow column of bricks which we hoped were not imporant in terms of propping up the rest of the building and the flats above. Masses of timber started to arrive and more holes appeared in various places, more or less where we expected them to be. Peter Church and his expensive joiners sat around doing odd jobs and waiting for the detailed drawings without which they could not start. We kept on chasing the architect who, being a hippy, talked about 'good vibes' and mouthed a lot of other platitudes that were getting us nowhere.

In a panic we realized that if we were to open at all we would have to call in another designer, so we rang Tony Little late one night and he came round straightaway. The electricity was not working and we stumbled around in the darkness explaining our problems. Tony said that we should have the advice of another architect and David Mainey arrived the next morning. While he was walking around the building he came to the original misplaced hole in the wall. He took one look and flicked it with his finger. There was a loud pinging noise and David went ashen. He leaped up the stairs and out on to the street. The crumbling column of bricks was meant to support the entire building. David immediately sent for a builder to reinforce the wall and refused to come near the shop until this had been done.

There were only six weeks to go before the shop was due to open. Our financial problems were such that any delay would have been a disaster. Peter Church and his joiners had been so held up that the only possible way they could finish on time was to work twenty-four hours a day. There were twelve of them, and any more would only get in each other's way.

One of the tenants of the flats above was the managing director of a big West End department store. He thought our workmen were deliberately disturbing him. Every night he would come down and make a commotion, threatening us with the police, his solicitors, and finally his next-door neighbour, whom he described as an ill-tempered giant who could eat Fitz for breakfast. Finally, one night, after another violent shouting match, he returned with his neighbour, who was indeed very large. The giant took one look at Fitz, put his arm around his shoulders and said, 'Hello there, you bastard – will you come up and have a drink?' He was Sean Treacy, an author, and landlord of the Queen's Elm, an old stamping ground for Fitz in his bachelor days. After that lucky chance we had no more interruptions at night and the work continued.

As we came to the last weekend it really started to seem that we would fail. The workmen were exhausted. Some of them had not been home for weeks, sleeping in any quiet nook that they could find. It was early September and the weather was very hot. The shop seemed to collect humidity and the sweaty marble floor was agony for tired feet. An atmosphere of wild desperation was developing. At the last minute we threw in the reserves. The forty beautiful sales-girls who were meant to start work on the Monday all volunteered to help and arrived en masse on Sunday morning. Kim had a boyfriend who was a member of a pop group. They all turned up as well. The street at the back of the shop was full of girls working with paint brushes. Our entire staff, pattern cutters, machinists, drivers and accounts clerks, were painting and pushing, cleaning and getting in each other's way. Boyfriends arrived to collect their girls and were immediately set to work. Fitz and I went round and round trying to organize this chaos.

At around 10 p.m. we sent the girls home so that they would be fit for the next day. The shop was still a building site: bits of timber and tools were everywhere. Workbenches and pots of paint covered the floor. Fitz took his team of pop musicians and started to throw every-thing on one huge pile on the pavement behind the shop. At the same time the cleaners arrived. It was nearly our undoing. To the workforce, addled by lack of sleep and just returned from a break in the pubs, the ten or so cleaning women had the impact of a chorus line. The women loved it. It was like a bacchanalian nightmare, with couples disappearing into stockrooms and locking themselves in the loos. Fitz looked in despair at Peter Church. 'What in hell do we do now?'

'Don't worry,' said Peter, 'it won't last.' And he was right. Soon sheepish faces started to appear and we were quickly back working at full blast.

At about 4 a.m. the pop group had finally thrown everything out on to the street and the time came to remove the hoardings from the front of the shop. Fitz and I went to the other side of the street to see what it looked like. Again we had forgotten about the name. It was beautiful. Dawn was breaking as we stumbled back to work.

As we were hanging the garments on hatstands we had to step over the bodies of sleeping workmen. The moment the job was over they lay down where they were and passed out. When the shop girls returned at 8 o'clock the place looked like the end of an orgy.

At the last minute Fitz noticed that the back door had not been painted. While he was painting it, looking really filthy, a man came up to him, looked at the huge pile of tools and equipment, and said, 'The man that owns this place is made of money. He just doesn't care – look at all this stuff he's thrown away. I'm coming back with my van.'

'Quite right, mate,' said Fitz.

When the shop opened in September 1969, it was an instant success. Over one hundred thousand people visited us every week. One Saturday the *Daily Mail* counted the number of customers who came through the doors. We had a bigger crowd than Queen's Park Rangers – thirty thousand. The *Sunday Times* called it 'the most beautiful store in the world'.

A short time after the opening of the High Street shop the first biggy paper acknowledged us. Prudence Glynn wrote an article in *The Times*. It was an enormous spread with beautiful pictures of Elly and other girls in our clothes, and of the new shop. The *Times* article attracted *Women's Wear Daily*, which published a double-page spread. You could see the funny side and charm in these pictures. The clothes were very serious and sombre, and the surroundings were old-fashioned, but they were being displayed by very young faces. The Kensington old ladies loved it. In the High Street our very first customer was an old lady in a flowered hat who made a beeline for the fringed lampshades. I thought, 'Oh God, we're doomed! Turn the music up.'

We were now developing all categories of clothing. In the basement area that Tony Little had transformed into a conservatory, with paper designed around the stained glass windows from St Paul's, was the underwear department. Knickers and bras were heaped into china wash bowls. The accessories stood on painted pub tables of different sizes. There were now two changing rooms to accommodate the crowds on Saturdays. One was mirrored entirely, decorated with peacock wallpaper cut-outs. The smaller changing room was done as a stage dressing room with little light bulbs around the mirror frames. The fitted carpet was a disaster. It didn't resemble the expected rich brown, but looked as if it had a layer of dust covering it. I needn't have worried. It would have looked like that anyway after a million feet had trodden on it.

Although Biba had begun as Art Nouveau, we never wished to ruin the original style of any premises. If the mouldings were Deco, they would stay Deco. Had we moved into a fifties' building I would not have altered its character. Once the pillars were revealed in the High Street shop, the place took on the original architect's intention. We sprayed them gold and Julie designed a beautiful border that followed the pillars round the perimeter of the whole of the ground floor.

The sumptuous cream and milkshake pink gallery was filled with more expensive, sequined dresses and long leather maxi coats. After a week the cream carpet looked awful and the pink walls were covered in black finger marks. It was a favourite place for hippies, who lolled on the velvet-covered chaise longues. Nobody approved of them but I always wanted outcasts or an odd tramp to be welcome. It was only when we discovered a used French letter amongst the cushions on the seat under the stairs that Fitz instructed the girls to keep everybody moving.

Children's clothes, too, were now an important part of Biba. At the very back of the shop a relatively small area was allocated to the kiddies. This time the ceiling was higher but it was still a very cosy little room. We had murals of fairies and gnomes painted all over the walls and ceilings. Kids stayed in there for hours, playing.

We had men's clothes in the basement and a household department by the front door. I had become very interested in household goods because, apart from antiques, it was impossible to buy anything that worked with Art Nouveau, Victorian or Edwardian furniture. All the things I needed, other people needed too. I hated buying cut flowers, I didn't like to see them die. Ostrich feathers dyed in different colours replaced flowers as decoration. Potted palms were now becoming very expensive, but they were so much a part of Biba that they were a must. Hatstands were difficult to find and their price had trebled. Before the Kensington High Street store opened, Fitz and I drove round London searching the antique shops for hatstands. We needed hundreds. We passed an antique shop with hatstands piled up on the pavement. Fitz stopped the car and rushed into the shop to ask the price. 'Fifteen pounds each,' was the reply. 'There's a rich idiot buying up all the hatstands in London for his new shop and he'll pay anything.'

'Oh yeah?' said Fitz.

In the end we had to resort to buying new ones, made in Czechoslovakia.

*

The counter nearest the door was for cosmetics. I had seen a film when I was thirteen that I never forgot, with Rita Gam as a slave girl. She hadn't looked made up but her lips had obviously been painted brown. I couldn't wait to have brown lipstick and other natural shades. Lips and nails had always been painted scarlet. I remembered my aunt telling me that nail varnish had become fashionable in the thirties in Brazil. It was worn to cover the white moon under your fingernails that gave away your mulatto blood.

We had found a factory near East Grinstead that produced cosmetics for all the big brands. When I showed them the colours we wanted for our lipsticks and nail varnish and eye colours, the managers didn't seem to take us seriously. On the other hand, the girls in the laboratory were terribly excited and couldn't wait to formulate something different from the usual corals and bright pinks. They stayed up all night and mixed our first ever brown lipstick, which sold out in the first half hour.

Our first foundation arrived in large vats from the factory and was poured into the bottles on our kitchen table by Del, Eva, and Witold's nanny. The customers loved it. They could play with make-up for as long as they liked. We were the first to encourage customers to experiment before they bought, and they made themselves at home. Some even came in very early in the morning with faces scrubbed clean, made themselves up and continued on to work.

After a few successful months it was decided that we would sell all over the country in the Dorothy Perkins shops, but first of all their manageresses had to be shown how to use the chocolate lipstick and mulberry eyeshadow, and how to secure the spidery fake eyelashes on to their lids. The blue-rinsed ladies arrived at the Bracknell warehouse from the provinces and after a happy lunch our girls showed them how to apply the make-up. By the time they reached the eyelashes there was chaos, but they all really enjoyed themselves.

After much thought we decided to give a press launch party for the make-up range. We gave a tea dance one Sunday afternoon in April 1970. The shop had been stripped of merchandise and the ground floor filled with round tables covered with cream lace tablecloths, decorated with giant candles and thousands of cream ostrich feathers.

Our girls were all decked out in long flowing crêpe and chiffon dresses, and we hired a hairdresser to make sure they all looked glamorous. We were using an outside catering contractor and dressed the waitresses in black dresses with frilly aprons and caps made in the workroom. We had plates of cakes and watercress and cucumber sandwiches (Fitz's favourite). There were seven different types of tea and a full bar. The centrepiece was a near lifesize cake of a Biba cosmetics girl with dropping lids and pouting chocolate mouth, which had been designed and made for us by our illustrator, Malcolm Bird. Downstairs in the basement the units designed by Whitmore Thomas, from which we were going to sell the cosmetics in the Dorothy Perkins shops, were all lined up, looking like a cross between dressing tables and Daleks. One of the changing rooms was converted into a party room for the crowds of children that we hoped would come. We had a professional clown to entertain them and Witold was waiting, his eyes shining with excitement, dressed as a Cossack.

We had hired a marvellous old-fashioned three-piece orchestra straight from the thirties, two women and a man. He had a slicked back hairstyle and was wearing full gigolo regalia, and we had made special white satin dresses for the women. Despite all the instructions about the mood of the afternoon and the 1930s' tea dance atmosphere that we wanted, our two shiny satin-clad violinists turned up sporting rather shabby fifties' bouffant hairdos, glistening with lacquer. It took all our tact and diplomacy to rush them to the hairdresser.

When all was ready we lined up to wait for our guests, Fitz and I by the door with the beauties behind us to act as usherettes. Outside was a huge awning covering the front of the shop, and underneath stood someone's boyfriend dressed in a thirties' chauffeur's uniform – high buttoned jacket, riding breeches, high boots and peaked cap – waiting to open the car doors. One really feels a fool at such moments. There you are, ready to go, all that money spent and about seventy people ready to spring into action, just waiting for the guests. A few years later, in the Rainbow Room in our last shop, we still had that feeling on our big nights, even though we had realized by then that everyone always comes later and they all come at once.

That's what happened that afternoon. The first two people to arrive were obviously gatecrashers but we were so relieved to see them that they were treated like royalty. Suddenly everyone else was there.

The boy in the uniform outside was leaping up and down the road opening doors. Swarms of people were queuing to get in. We were interviewed by the *Financial Times* on one side and the *Daily Mirror* on the other. The BBC *Nationwide* team arrived with lorries and cables and cameras everywhere. Twiggy turned up and, with her usual lack of affectation, started to play with the dozens of children running wild downstairs.

Soon, dishevelled people were tripping over television cables, the basement floor was awash with drink and everybody was laughing and shouting. The party was a success. When people started to leave they took handfuls of the expensive ostrich feathers with them, to our dismay. We had to let them – to have asked for them back would have ruined the atmosphere that we had achieved.

Finally we were alone with our staff and started the long task of putting the shop back into shape for the next day. However the fun was not yet over. The hired waitresses had obviously been helping themselves to the drinks and it suddenly began to show. The shop rang with the noise of breaking china and crashing trays. This was really very funny – it was *their* china, not ours – but things became out of hand when the lady in charge seized hold of a dangerous-looking bread knife and started slashing about her. We had to disarm her and Peter Church and the store detective frogmarched her into the street, where she began to hammer on the windows, which were fortunately made of bulletproof glass.

At last the owner of the catering company arrived, but far from being contrite he started to go for Fitz for insulting his wife who, it transpired, was the lady with the knife. By this time we had had enough of them all, so he was removed too and joined his wife on the pavement.

The very next day the launch of the new-look Dorothy Perkins shop in Oxford Street was held. We were there because it was the first time that our cosmetics were to be sold outside our own four walls. We arrived about forty minutes before the press were due and could not believe our eyes when we saw that our beautiful cosmetics unit had a smashed mirror that had been partly disguised by a poster stuck on crookedly. I remember furiously asking a Dorothy Perkins director what had happened. He came back with the classic response, 'It broke last night and I made an executive decision!' Every time since then when Fitz and I want to describe a really stupid idea to each other we say, 'He made an executive decision.' There is another phrase we use that was taken from one of my brothers-in-law, when he was our production manager. Explaining why he left the whole production schedule in a complete muddle when he went on holiday, he said, 'My plan was perfect – but the factories let me down.' Now, when Fitz says, 'My plan was perfect', I know that something has gone badly wrong.

Fitz didn't want me to do footwear, but we found an English factory and sampled a pair of boots. The first time round the factory got them right. They were knee length suede with a shaped heel that was much higher than was fashionable at the time. Later Daphne told me she thought I had gone too far. The heel was 3 inches high and today it looks like a pig's trotter. The leg was zipped up the side so tightly that it impeded the flow of blood. I had great trouble convincing Fitz that we should order them but the first delivery of five hundred pairs sold out in two days.

Queues formed daily, watching for delivery of the boots. It didn't matter which colour came in, people would buy it and then come back for another colour the next day. When a delivery arrived at the back door, Janice, who had just joined us and was put on the boot counter, would call out size and colour. We sold the boots for £8 19s. 6d. In three months we sold seventy-five thousand pairs. The shoe trade, we were told later, would come at night and count the empty boxes outside the back door to see how many had been sold that day. The telephone never stopped ringing for information about colour and size.

One Saturday afternoon I managed to drag Fitz down to the Kings Road into Antiquarius, the antique market. Fitz was unhappy to be away from the shop. He left me at a stall and said he was going to telephone them. He came running back, white-faced, stuffed some money into my hand for a taxi and said, 'Now don't worry, there's a bomb in the shop,' and shot off.

He had asked Irene if everything was all right.

'Yes,' she said. 'It's fine, but there has been a bomb scare.'

'What do you mean?' asked Fitz.

'Well, this geezer said we had ten minutes to go before it went off, and then he rang again and said we had five minutes.'

'Do as I say, Irene,' said Fitz. 'Blow smoke into the fire alarm to make it go off and clear the shop.'

I was left in Antiquarius with a couple of pound notes in my hand. I rushed out and caught a taxi. By the time I reached the shop, crowds of customers were out on the pavement and so were all the staff. I couldn't see Fitz. Someone said the bomb had gone off. I died a thousand deaths before I reached the front door.

Inside, Fitz and the manageress were inspecting the damage. The police had arrived. They said it was lucky there hadn't been sugar in the bomb, as the whole shop would then have been set alight. Half the basement was demolished. There were bits of hatstands all over the place.

The man who had telephoned the shop got on to a dizzy dolly who had automatically said, 'Today we have mulberry and bluebottle, sizes 4, $4^{1/2}$ and 6 only.'

He'd said to her, 'You've got ten minutes before a bomb will go off.' She only repeated her message and put the receiver down.

By now the man was desperate. He dialled again and got another report on the boot situation. By now he was yelling down the phone, 'This is serious, you have only five minutes!'

It was the first time a bomb had been planted in a public place in London. Previously the targets had been the houses of MPs and other public figures. Later we discovered it was the Angry Brigade who were responsible for the explosion. The Angry Brigade were a group of anarchists loosely connected with the women's movement. Their decision to blow us up, which came out at their trial, was based on the following crazy reasoning: women are slaves to fashion, Biba leads fashion, therefore blowing up Biba will liberate women.

After this our telephone was continually busy with nutters threatening us. One lot called themselves 'The Guerrillas of Great Britain'. One Saturday afternoon I had just washed my hair and coaxed it into huge rollers. I got a call from the shop to say there was another scare and that I should leave the house. I rushed upstairs to get Witold. I told his nanny to grab the dogs. We piled into the car and drove round the block. I found the nearest telephone box and called the shop. There was no answer. God, I thought, they're all dead. I drove round to the High Street, where there was a huge crowd on the pavement. I could see a few of our girls but not Fitz. I left the restless brood in the car and as I reached the crowd I heard a woman say, 'It's just another publicity stunt.' I nearly hit her.

I still couldn't see Fitz. There were fire engines outside. The girls told me Fitz was inside. The firemen had told him to send the girls into the shop to search for the bomb! If he is in there I am going in as well, I thought. I found them but Fitz, Peter Church and Gary, our Saturday security man, told me to get out. They were searching everything, looking for a bomb without knowing what it looked like. It's an awful feeling not knowing if a bra you are handling is going to go bang in your face. Every pocket of all the garments had to be examined because some bombs are no larger than a pencil. That time it was just a scare.

The cosmetics went off like a rocket. In some places our little unit was taking over 10 per cent of the total sales of the entire shop. Almost immediately we started to sell in other countries. Elio Fiorucci asked to launch our cosmetics in Italy, through his shop in Milan. We arrived there with six of our girls. The cosmetics by now included blue, green, purple and black lipstick, with matching eyeshadows and contour powder for the cheeks. Wherever the girls went there was silence. Elly was completely blue: blue make-up, blue clothes, blue cap and blue curls. Eva was all green, Del all violet. Some girls were all in black, looking like Dracula. Elio and Christina Fiorucci asked us to lunch at the Torre di Pisa. The girls arrived in their full regalia looking as if they had just left a Fellini set, and ate and drank. When we left we all piled into taxis to go to the Fiorucci shop. Elly, in a blue haze entered a taxi that was already taken. We watched the astonished passenger's face as she made herself comfortable next to him. I think he was wondering if he had the DTs.

Our coloured wigs became an important accessory. My aunt had told me how when she went on long journeys to India she would have a little row of false curls to use when her hair was not in the right condition. She would put on a close fitting cap, stuff the curls round the edge, and presto – she would look her immaculate self again. I had similar curls made on a piece of wire but for Biba they were dipped into lots of unnatural colours – navies, violets, mulberry and bright henna. They proved very useful on photographic sessions to cut down on hairdressing time.

At about this time Dorothy Perkins bought out the other partners and now had the majority shareholding. Our lack of experience in the cosmetics business made us fall into many traps. The most dramatic was caused by the company that filled a very beautiful decanter with our cologne. We did not know that the liquid expanded in heat and so a bottle should not be filled to the brim. The first sign of trouble was when the girl representing us in California, the first place to become hot that summer, rang us to say that all her bottles had burst. Before we could work out why, there were calls coming in from all over the world. Our entire distribution was reeking of old tomcat as thirty thousand bottles exploded.

Just as we were really getting going we found ourselves in another near disastrous situation. As usual it was caused by the complacency of professional executives. It was decided by David Roxburgh that we should have a general manager to take charge of the cosmetics administration. He found someone from his head office, and together they played at being miniature Charles Revsons. The first hint I had of a problem was when Del Howard, who was in charge of sampling, rang the Bracknell clerks with an order from me. She was told that we could not sample any more new colours because we were over our budget. Angry and perplexed, I stormed into Fitz's office, only to find that according to his calculations we were in fact under-stocked.

By now we were both thoroughly alarmed and the next morning Fitz went with Del down to Bracknell to see what was up. To his horror Fitz found that £2 million more of orders had been placed than he had estimated would sell in the next five years. White-faced, he went to David Roxburgh and told him the news. In fact they had gone completely out of control. The magnitude of the error was such that it could have brought down the whole Dorothy Perkins empire as well as ourselves.

The entire Biba accounts department was working sixteen hours a day to analyse exactly what the position was. It was unbelievable – in the first two months of our relatively small business we had bought more lipstick than Revlon and Max Factor combined. Fitz was rushing round the suppliers, cancelling, threatening and buying drinks, trying to reduce the vast commitments that had been made in our name without losing the trust and respect of the cosmetics industry.

Fitz hired someone to help him control the future production himself. He explained the situation gently to the new man so as not to alarm him. When Fitz revealed the colossal amounts that had been delivered, starting with fifteen years' worth of moisturizer, thirty years' supply of shampoo and a really impressive 150 years' supply of hand creams, all the new man could say was, 'Christ, this stuff goes off, you know!' which must be some sort of record for understatement.

St Tropez was an important outlet for our cosmetics. At that time it still had a great magic. Our first delivery was made by an old friend of ours, Dennis Morgan, a big, jolly Irishman who had helped us many times in the past when only great physical effort would get us out of a mess. Dennis set off in one of his trucks, loaded with display units and stock. He had never heard of export licences and all the bureaucratic traps into which one always falls. Somehow Dennis managed to pass the Calais customs without a problem but unfortunately he was arrested in Marseille. His van was impounded and he was put in the local jail. He was allowed the statutory one telephone call, but we were abroad and it took him three days to get through to Fitz. It took another three days to get Dennis released, but he made up for it once he reached St Tropez. A friend of ours was there at the same time and told us stories of a lunatic Irishman setting a new fashion in Marks and Spencer vests, leading a gang of tearaways around the precious atmosphere of the boutiques and restaurants of the port.

Finally the problem was brought under control and we decided to expand the cosmetics to other countries. As Fitz and I both love the sun we would fly off to some warm place for a long weekend, setting up a cosmetics distribution in between bouts of sunbathing. By 1973 we were selling in over thirty countries, nearly all of them, coincidentally, with beautiful beaches.

Later in 1970 we launched our cosmetics in a department store in Japan. It had taken us nearly a year of negotiating with the Mitsubishi organization, but when they finally went on sale they were a big success and Japan became one of our most important markets.

The one country that you do not go rushing into is the USA. The market is very tough indeed and you really have to wait for your opportunity. Fortunately for us Rosemary McMurtney, the editor of the influential *Seventeen* magazine, with a circulation of several million copies a month, came to us in London suggesting that we should sell our clothes in America. If we managed the distribution she would do a feature on us. We really didn't want to become wholesalers; it is a different sort of business and one that we thought would be bad for our image. Instead we agreed that we would sell Biba prints to Macy's and that we would make up some special designs, selling the patterns through the McCall's pattern catalogue. This sounded ambitious but with Rosemary and *Seventeen* behind us it was really very simple. The clothes were photographed by Sarah Moon in a marvellous round 1920s' tower in the Au Printemps store in Paris. The results were truly beautiful and *Seventeen* gave us several pages of spectacular pictures.

In America they really understand about designers and the importance of maintaining their creative image right down to the last detail. Macy's actually asked us to design their full-page advertisement in the *New York Times*, and I sent detailed drawings showing how I wanted their window displays to look. We went to New York for the promotion and were amazed at how closely they had followed our instructions. It was more Biba than Biba.

We were looking for a major store to launch our cosmetics and Rosemary put us in touch with Colette Touhey, a young fashion buyer for the very upmarket Bergdorf Goodman store on Fifth Avenue right beside the Plaza Hotel. Colette is a really go-ahead buyer with a strong personality and over breakfast at the Plaza she convinced us that we should launch a small version of Biba on the sixth floor of Bergdorf Goodman. Fitz and I were both fairly hung-over and as we drove to the airport we looked at each other and said, 'What on earth have we done? We have just agreed to do exactly the opposite of what we planned.'

Whitmore Thomas built a special display unit in London and tried it out in the centre of the shop. It seemed to work so we rang New York, and Colette Touhey flew over. At the time there was a great rush for Biba boots and she stood spellbound, watching the silent queue waiting for the next delivery.

The unit and stock were shipped to New York in October 1970 and Fitz, Elly and I went over to set it up. We had agreed that there should always be one Biba girl from London working at Bergdorf to make sure that everything was being done exactly right, and Elly was the obvious choice to be the first. It was a delight to work with the people at Bergdorf Goodman. In those days it was still owned by the original

Andrew Goodman. There was to be an enormous publicity campaign, and the Goodmans were giving their first press luncheon for ten years in their own apartment.

The night before, Fitz and I and the entire Bergdorf display team were decorating all eight of the windows. The display team was about fifteen strong and each of them had brought a friend. Fitz and I were outside at about two in the morning, freezing in our fur coats in the middle of an ice storm, trying to direct by sign language where the various things should go. When we went back inside the floor was covered in black felt. Four people had spent hours pressing and smoothing it to make it ready for display. Mr Goodman had joined us and strolled up and down, dropping cigar ash and leaving footmarks on their night's work as he told some anecdote. They were all too scared of him to protest.

By the time we had finished overseeing the windows there was no point in going to bed so we went back to the Plaza, had a bath and returned to the store. The Goodmans' apartment occupied the entire top floor of the Bergdorf building, which is listed. When we arrived, Mrs Goodman showed us around. The bar was late thirties with Chinese lacquer walls covered in zebra skin. One living room was the length of the Ritz lobby. You could barely see the far end. There were giant fireplaces and elegant sofas arranged in clusters down the length of the room. Even Auntie would have been silenced by its size. The most interesting part was the black bathroom, which is featured in most books on Art Deco. Even the scales embedded in the floor were black marble. The dial was set at eye level so there was no way you could cheat.

All that night Fitz had been boring me by rehearsing his speech for the big press lunch next day. Fitz is nervous at the best of times, and the thought of goofing up the entire East Coast fashion press at one go really had him worried. Mr Goodman spoke brilliantly and flatteringly for twenty minutes. Then there was a silence as Fitz got to his feet. I cannot remember what he said and nor can he. It lasted less than a minute, but he certainly got to them. They all stood up and gave him a terrific round of cheering and clapping, and the man next to me said, 'He sure is good on his feet!'

And that was that. In the first week we took an enormous $30,000 and the whole thing ran on sweetly. It worked because there was trust between both sides. Each week Colette would telex what she had sold and we would ring her and tell her what we could send that would keep her stock at the right level. She never queried what it looked like or how much it was and we never sent her anything that we knew was not right for her. It was a unique relationship and lasted until we opened our last big store, two years later.

Once Bergdorf Goodman was our flagship, other American stores started to want our things. To reproduce the Bergdorf scene anywhere else would have stretched our resources too much, so we would only sell them our cosmetics. The first store we went to was Bloomingdale's in New York. It is the number one cosmetics store in the world and the president, Marvin Traube, and head cosmetics buyer, Mike Blumenfelt, were extremely helpful to us.

With things going well on the East Coast we decided to try for the West. Several times in the course of conversation with American cosmetics people, the name of Marcia Israel, a legendary success in the American rag trade, had come up. The general theory was that if we were to make it in Los Angeles we would have to do a deal with her and that she would eat us alive. One day in London Fitz said, 'Bugger it! Let's ring her up and tell her we're coming to see her.' Thirty seconds later he was talking to her husband, Larry, and three days after that we were in Los Angeles for the first time.

We stayed in a bungalow at the Beverly Hills Hotel. There were film stars in the foyer. Witold, who was then three, would come rushing up boggle eyed to tell us which of his heroes he'd just seen. The night we were due to see the legendary Marcia a huge chauffeur-driven Cadillac drew up to the hotel, and swept us up to a huge and beautiful house high up in Beverly Hills. As the bronze Cadillac drew up at the portico, a matching bronze-coloured chicken greeted us. We entered the white marble hall. I had not seen a house as immaculate as this since my aunt's suite. There were no chipped mouldings, no cleverly sealed cracks in the walls. The rooms were unblemished and the restored antiques looked brand new.

Larry Israel, short and smiling, with blond-white hair and a brown face, was waiting to meet us and we were ushered through a real Hollywood film star house to meet one of the most charming and relaxed women I have ever encountered. Marcia said the house looked a mess. I smiled to myself – she should see what a mess really looks like. Outside the French windows there was a perfect Olympic-sized swimming pool filled with sparkling David Hockney water. A Frank Sinatra record was playing on the stereo system throughout the garden. But where was Esther Williams?

After a few pleasantries I was talking to Larry at the bar while he poured drinks. I heard to my horror Fitz and Marcia already slugging it out on the business front. Within two minutes they were into percentages, lead times and stock back-up. Five minutes later they shook hands and it was all over. We had travelled six thousand miles to do a deal that the experts had said was impossible, and it was done in seven minutes. It was a great deal for both sides and lasted without a single harsh word, until we finally parted company with Biba.

After that we all went off to dinner and Fitz and I sat fascinated by Larry and Marcia's tales of Hollywood. They knew everything and everyone and with their introduction into the Hollywood scene we quickly found our way around. To me, despite all the tales of heart-break and harshness, it is still the most unbelievably interesting and glamorous place. I love it. The next few days we spent with Twiggy and Michael Whitney, her fiancé, star peeping around the pool of the Beverly Hills Hotel.

Soon after we arrived home we left our rambling house in Brunswick Gardens and moved to a big studio house near Holland Park. As our home life consisted of collapsing into bed at night and a hurried coffee in the morning, we converted it into a de luxe bedsitter so that everything was conveniently on the same level. Witold and his nanny had a world of their own downstairs.

Chapter Eight

In 1967, in the midst of a crisis, I had told our bank manager that Biba would one day be like Harrods. He gave me a long, puzzled look and said, 'Do you really want that?' I was adamant.

Each day as I walked from the Church Street shop to the new site in Kensington High Street, I had examined the Derry and Toms department store building close by. It was so beautiful and so un-appreciated. No one there had any respect for the building or its superb detail. It had been a star in its heyday but now as it grew old and dusty no one even gave it a glance. I began to daydream that one day we would bring it back to its original splendour. Many of the assis-tants had been there since its opening day and were now over sixty. I tried to imagine our girls at that age, with white hair entwined into plaits around their heads or coils around their ears.

Later, when the High Street shop was open, I noticed a tree on the roof of Derry and Toms, and realized there was a roof garden. One lunchtime in 1969, when Witold came to the shop with his nanny, the sun was shining and I said, 'Let's go up and see this "garden in the sky".' We walked over to the store and got into the rickety lift that went straight up to the roof.

We stepped out into another world – a most beautiful, well-kept garden. Somebody clearly adored and cared for it, although it had few flowers. We walked around the corner and there was another garden. Witold ran on to the little wooden bridge that crossed a narrow stream and we played Billy Goats Gruff for a while and then went on to exam-ine the tatty-looking flamingoes. We felt a million miles away from the noisy street below. Looking over the balustrade we could see the whole skyline of London around us.

'Fitz, one day we must have this place,' I said.

'Right, I'll get it for you,' he replied.

If you want something badly enough for long enough your wish will come true – often just as you have given up hoping. We had many wild dreams. Our problem was that they always came true a fraction too early. You can accomplish the impossible when you don't look back and stop to think twice about what you are on the point of tackling. As you grow older it becomes more difficult. But I knew that one day Derry's would be ours.

For the next two years I collected bits of furniture, cuttings of old carpets, mouldy old curtains with interesting weaves, and books and references about Derry and Toms. Any information that I might later need would be at my fingertips. I also collected people who would be useful for the big moment. They all had to be tested to see if they could deliver the goods and not just talk. Although I designed all the clothes for Biba, we used other designers for details like appliqué. Malcolm Bird did illustrations for the shop, David Musson did intarsia designs for jumpers and sequin appliqués. We bought in fabric designs for printing furnishing and dress fabrics. Anyone who was original was commissioned to do something specific for Biba. These decisions were principally my responsibility. The most successful wallpaper prints were by Suzy Sheradshi who later drew wallpaper and carpet designs for the first floor at Big Biba and for the Rainbow Room, derived from the old swatches I had collected. Daphne supervised the repeats and technical details on the designs.

Myra Conin spent two years mixing up the basic colours for all sorts of designs. Sometimes she would spend days mixing a brown until it was the correct shade we needed for a carpet. Eventually one could describe a colour to her verbally and she would be able to put it down on paper. She spent months decorating the thirties' bust that was duplicated in fibreglass throughout the big shop.

Seventy per cent of the things in Big Biba were manufactured by us. The rest were goodies we had found at fairs and obscure manufacturers. Once the word was out all the manufacturers that had been sitting on old stock in their attics came forward – there was jewellery, pottery and furniture.

We felt shocked when we heard that our dream was going to be either shattered or forced upon us earlier than we imagined. After all, we had only just moved to the High Street. By chance the head of the PR agency we used actually knew Sir Hugh Fraser, chairman of Derry and Toms, and heard that he was planning to sell. She organized a dinner party at her house in Windsor and invited Sir Hugh and us. It was a very high-powered party. Literally over the port and cigars

Fitz managed to bring up the subject of Derry and Toms. Was Sir Hugh really selling? Sir Hugh was not sure. Would Sir Hugh give us first option if he decided to sell? He might and he might not, but we left the party with the distinct impression that the building was available if we could raise the money.

The next step was to sell the idea to our partners. Fitz went to Bracknell, armed with reams of figures, to persuade the Dorothy Perkins board. We had agreed that come what may we were going to have that building, and if the answer was 'no' from Bracknell we had flights booked the next day for New York, where we had connections who might back us. But Dorothy Perkins agreed.

The next stage was a formal lunch at Claridge's with Sir Hugh Fraser. David Roxburgh and John Ritblat were there representing Dorothy Perkins. John Ritblat was the head of a huge property company, British Land, who were property advisers to Dorothy Perkins, and took charge of the negotiations. The lunch dragged on with Ritblat and Fraser telling stories about the deals that they had done. At the end of it everyone said goodbye and nothing seemed to have been accomplished.

One Friday afternoon at about 4 o'clock Fitz heard a rumour that the building was about to be sold to someone else. He rang Roxburgh, who called Ritblat on another line, and both said that there was no more that they could do. The deal was lost. Fitz was cursing Sir Hugh Fraser. 'He bloody promised it to us.'

'Ring him up,' I suggested.

Sir Hugh was at his desk in Glasgow. Fitz said, 'I hear you are selling the building.'

'Yes,' said Sir Hugh.

'You promised it to us,' said Fitz.

'Have you got £3.9 million?'

'Yes,' said Fitz, who had no idea how far Dorothy Perkins might go.

'Stay by your phone,' said Sir Hugh.

Two minutes later a call came through to Fitz from the director in charge of the House of Fraser in London. It was very dramatic. 'I can't talk loud,' he said. 'I have British Home Stores with me and I am about to sign with them. Sir Hugh tells me that he has sold to you. I must have £400,000 in my hands by tonight.'

Fitz went a bit white but promised it would be with him in one and a half hours. He rang Roxburgh with the news. Roxburgh was speechless but passed it on to Ritblat who arranged the transfer of the money within the hour.

Although we had been planning the store together in great depth for months, once the excitement had died down we started to realize the enormity of what we had done. The sheer size of the building and the number of detailed drawings that had to be produced before a single workman set foot on the site were daunting. We had eighteen months before the House of Fraser moved out and then only twelve weeks of actual working time to make the transformation.

The original idea was that the Dorothy Perkins architects' department would be in charge of the practical side of the work while we concentrated on how the store would look. After a few weeks it became obvious that their experience in organizing three hundred small shops had little relevance to putting together a department store of 400,000 square feet. Everything we wanted seemed to cost two or three times as much as we had anticipated and our budget of £1 million, which had seemed more than enough to do what we wanted, suddenly looked as if it would cover only the absolute basics like electricity, plumbing, and reconditioning the lifts, leaving virtually nothing for the facelift that our customers would actually see.

Our first thought was to split the task up, giving each floor to a different designer, but we were frightened of starting something so huge with people whose abilities we did not really know. We decided that we would stay with the Whitmore Thomas team and strengthen them by employing back-up draughtsmen, all working under our control.

Fitz could see that with only the DP architects to help him he had no chance of ever opening the doors. He decided to form his own team of experts so that he could have complete control of the budget and programming, as I had of the design. He came across a professional project manager called Peter Trotter. Our first meeting was, to say the least, stormy. Trotter stood for everything that I disliked. He was large, overbearing and treated me, as a designer, with sickening condescension, but he obviously knew the business. After the meeting Fitz said to me, 'Look I know he's a right bastard but that's what we need.'

We also hired the John Grasemark film design studio to support

Whitmore Thomas and we moved the whole lot into a big room on the ground floor of our offices. We had just moved into a new and much bigger office and warehouse building by the Regent's Canal, and in order to have complete control we set up a design studio on the ground floor. It was perfect. I had my team working in the merchandise department on the first floor and the designers drawing away below. In the same way Fitz had his merchandise controllers, who made sure that everything was running on budget, plus his building team, all on the premises. Peter Trotter had introduced Sammy Leigh, a quantity surveyor. Before Fitz committed one penny of the budget, he and Sammy and Peter went through all the plans of how the store was to be laid out and set a price for everything. From 55,000 feet of marble, through carpet and display units, down to tills and computer terminals and plug points and electric light bulbs, everything was priced.

Floor by floor and section by section we briefed the designers and draughtsmen. I have found that the only way to get exactly what you want from creative people is to brief them down to the most minute detail so that no time is wasted on airy fairy theorizing and everyone knows exactly what is expected of them. We couldn't afford to repeat our previous mistakes. Another thing that we had learned was never to allow experts to take control. The fact that they are specialists in a particular subject means that their vision is narrowed and they resist all attempts to adapt. For example, our budget for electrics was £100,000 and that was that. The expert came up with a plan that would have cost twice this amount. Fitz explained that we only had £100,000 and that was that. The expert said it was impossible so Fitz sent for another, and another, until he had what he wanted at the price we could afford. Once everyone understood how we worked and accepted the disciplines that this entailed, things started to roll.

We were having our display units made all over the United Kingdom. They were delivered in sections and assembled in a huge warehouse in Bracknell. We would go down early most mornings and see that everything was as we had expected. Anything slightly wrong was put right on the spot. Anything ghastly and the whole thing was sent back. Once we had approved it, it was stripped down again to its component pieces, and stored ready to be delivered to London at the appropriate time.

The quantities involved were enormous and we had to check everything – we could leave nothing to chance. We had bought a mountain of beige marble in Portugal for the ground floor. We didn't realize that the colour of marble changes the deeper into the mountain you get. When Daphne and I went to the quarry we had to sort the colours into batches so that it could be laid in such a way that no one would notice the difference. We only had fourteen weeks' work on the site, and with the publicity and advertising already committed it would have been impossible to put back the opening day.

We were so absorbed in the future that we had been paying little attention to what was going on in the High Street Ken. shop. The first hint of trouble was an article in the *Guardian* saying that the Biba shop girls were trying to join the trade union USDAW and that we had threatened to sack them if they did. Fitz and I immediately went to the shop and spoke to Elly, who was now manageress. It was the first that she had heard of it. But the atmosphere in the shop was terrible. The girl who appeared to be ringleader of a small group of troublemakers was someone we had good reason to suspect of stealing from us. Of course, we couldn't do anything to stop her now, as any accusation we made would have been called victimization. A journalist on the *Guardian* was a friend of one of this group and to us he seemed to be orchestrating the whole thing. A few days later the *Guardian* ran another story, saying that the girls were going to walk out and stage a march down the High Street. Perhaps, if you are a young girl and keep reading that you are dissatisfied and exploited, in the end you will begin to believe it. Overnight we had a real problem.

The Dorothy Perkins board wanted nothing to do with such an unseemly business and Fitz was left to cope with the whole sorry mess. Finally the officials of USDAW asked for a meeting with him. The union delegation was headed by a really nice man. Fitz asked him what was wrong, and what complaints the girls had. Mr White replied that they didn't have any complaints. They weren't asking for more money or shorter hours or better conditions.

'So what's all the fuss?' asked Fitz.

Mr White said he thought that they were uncertain as to their future in the big store. Fitz explained that we were uncertain about *our* future if we were going to have this sort of problem without

Top Left/Bottom
**Favourite model
Stephanie Farrow exemplifies
the changing Biba face**
Hans Feurer

Top Right
Biba Country Tweeds
Sarah Moon

Top Left/Bottom Left
Luxurious lounges, little hats
and an Art Deco revival

Top Right
Drawing from the Biba
Colouring Book
K. Charko

Bottom Right
Sarah Moon in front of a
Julie Hodgess window front
of High Street Kensington

Top/Bottom
Twiggy displays the opulence
and style of Big Biba
Justin de Villeneuve

Left
The classic celtic Biba logo
designed by John McConnell

Right
The main entrance of Big Biba
Philip Sayer

Top
Twiggy in the Rainbow room,
Big Biba

Justin de Villeneuve

Bottom
Luxury on the gallery,
Kensington High Street

Sarah Moon

Top Left
Othello

Top Right
Aunt Sophie in 1955

Bottom Left
Witold impersonates
Mick Jagger

Bottom Right
Barbara, Witold and
Stephen Fitz-Simon in 1972
Desmond O'Neill

Top
The team: key members of the
staff for the opening of Big Biba
including Aina with the pageboy
haircut, Eleanor Powell in the
leopard skin dress, Delicia
Howard in the top hat, Joyce

O'Toole as a cigarette girl
and Uriah with Othello
Rolph Gobbits

Bottom
The Derry and Toms building

Fitz and Barbara at home,
Holland Park

James Wedge

apparent reason. We actually had no objection to recognizing the union; what we did object to was having a dishonest person as its leader. That problem was resolved when the girl in question got drunk one night and started boasting of the money she was stealing from the till and how powerless we were to do anything about it. She must have realized what she had done, because two days later she disappeared. The union leadership passed to a statuesque blonde Lithuanian called Aina, and her friend Gunda.

In the early days of the union there was great suspicion between the shop manageresses and the union committee. Irene, Elly and Kim, in particular, felt that their authority was being undermined by a new group of leaders who had direct access to Fitz and me. We did our best to heal the wounds, and Aina and Gunda and the rest became a tower of strength to us later.

One afternoon in the summer of 1972 Fitz came to my desk carrying a copy of the *Evening Standard* and looking very white. The headline on the city page carried the announcement that Dorothy Perkins had been taken over by British Land.

The shock was awful. It is every retailer's nightmare to be controlled by a property developer. The two have interests that are totally at loggerheads. The landlord must get the maximum rent while the shopkeeper must fight for every last penny. Furthermore as we read the article we saw that the Farmer family, with whom we had worked so happily for five years, was going to leave the company and control was passing to a board of directors composed of two accountants, a personnel manager, and someone from an advertising agency. There was not one retailer amongst them. It was going to be an impossible situation.

We both knew that the right thing for us personally to do was to resign at that moment. Biba was still at its peak: we would have been financially very well off indeed, and we could have walked away and let them get on with it. On the other hand, Biba was our child and to desert her now was impossible. We knew that from that day forward we would have a fight to the end on our hands which we could only win with our optimism and energy.

Just before we had taken possession of the site, Fitz, who had been testing 25 per cent proof English wine, tripped and broke his left ankle badly. It was a big blow because our plans had called for him to be charging round the building all day long and now he was in great pain even when he was sitting down. For the first few weeks he spent his time being wheeled round in an invalid chair.

The first day of the building work was really impressive. Before we could start we had to clear out all the rubbish and bits of odd shop-fitting left behind by Derry and Toms. We had more than six hundred men in the building on that first day. Over half of them appeared to have worked for us at some time or other in the past. Shouts of 'Hello, Barbara' followed me as I walked about between the heaps of debris. As the rubbish was cleared it was wildly exhilarating to see revealed for the first time the beautiful Art Deco details of the building.

Before we had finished the children's floor and the food hall, both of which I wanted to be fantasy worlds, there were two places that I felt I had to see: Disneyland and New Orleans. I particularly wanted to see them through Witold's eyes. He was now five years old and his reaction was very important to help clarify my own ideas. We went on a lightning trip. New Orleans was disappointing – it had been heavily commercialized and become very tacky. But Disneyland in California was absolutely marvellous. So much feeling and detail had been put into it. The only thing that jarred the fantasy were the crude remarks from the humans inside the giant Disney figures. I had become separated from the others and was chatted up by Pluto, who quickly became amorous. If he was crude, Minnie Mouse was obscene and made a pass at me in the middle of Main Street. I went puce with embarrassment. I tried to look into her matt fibreglass eyes. Minnie wasn't female. Only Witold's appearance stopped her lurid language. In the meantime Fitz had heard the tail end of my brush with Pluto. He was really furious and wanted to go and hit him. I could imagine what would happen to the man who punched Pluto on the nose. He would have been torn to pieces by thousands of fans that were lining the sidewalks. I seized Witold and Fitz by the arm and marched them both off as quickly as possible in the direction of the Haunted House.

We were only away for four days and when we returned the work on the building was going well. The only thing that was not functioning was the computer that was meant to tell us exactly where we were. Sammy Leigh had produced 1000 pages of minute calculations which Fitz by this time virtually knew by heart. Every evening he would spend hours with Peter Trotter working out where our budget was overrunning and what we could reduce or eliminate if we were not to overspend. Then Fitz and I would discuss options in his office on the fifth floor behind the Rainbow Room. Every day the situation changed as unexpected complications and problems emerged. We had not been able to do a proper survey of the building before we started work, because Derry's were trading up to the last moment, so no one really knew what the builders would find until they had a chance to open it up. On the whole we were very lucky, and the people we employed were very skilled.

The only thing that really took us aback was the attitude of the fire brigade. We had always been terrified of fire and had taken more than the legal minimum precautions in all our shops. Biba was the first department store to open in London since just after World War II, and everybody was throwing the rule book at us. We were as concerned as anybody that the store should be completely safe, but the fire brigade went to extraordinary lengths to interfere with what we were doing before we were open to the public. As stockrooms became completed and lockable, merchandise began to arrive and with it the manageresses and stockroom people. We had three hundred skilled craftsmen and a further three hundred of our own people working in the building. There were two back staircases, one on either side of the building, which ran the full 130 feet from basement to roof garden. At each entrance on every floor there was a fire door and the rule was that these doors should always be closed. But there were people passing through them the entire time, usually carrying something heavy, and the natural temptation was to wedge the doors open. Whenever the fire officer appeared and found a door that was not closed, which was about twice a day, he would threaten to shut the entire building, and he had the power to do so.

Fitz posted a small team of girls on the top floor. As soon as the fireman was spotted the security men would radio up and Fitz and the girls and anyone else who was in the office would go charging down the stairs shutting doors. It was stupid, but the threat of being closed before we were open was real and became an obsession with everybody.

At last the moment had come when I had to start laying out the merchandise. Fitz had worked out a schedule floor by floor and department by department for when the shopfitting would be complete and the merchandise in the stockrooms. I had six weeks and over 100,000 square feet of shop, and I was the only person who could do it. As I had designed or bought each thing, I had a mental picture of how they would all work together, and it was impossible to transmit the overall impression to others.

The huge display units had all arrived from the Bracknell warehouse. They were reassembled in their final places and the finishing touches applied. As each department was finished, the manageresses and stockroom workers would assemble a cross section of all the stock around me and I would start to work.

The first department to be ready we called the Casbah. It was on the front corner of the ground floor and comprised all the things that we had picked up and seen on our travels from Turkey via Beirut to Morocco. At about 6.30 one night the store had gone quiet; the workmen had left and there was an enormous silence. Through the brown paper-covered windows I could hear the traffic and the life outside. There was a busking bagpiper playing outside Barker's, the store across the street. According to Fitz's schedule I only had until 1 a.m. to complete this part, and after I had worked for two hours lifting heavy brass objects, I seemed to have been going backwards. Fitz was at one of his meetings and could not come to help me for at least another hour. The manageresses and stock controllers were still working, but so involved in their own problems of checking everything and entering it on to the forms for the computer that they would all be exhausted before their day was over.

My back was aching, and I felt completely lost. I had 130,000 square feet to go and was already tired out and way behind on the first 1000. I had been vaguely aware of two girls sitting near me, watching what I was doing. As I wearily approached another large brass pot, one of them walked over and lifted it before I could get there.

'Are you OK, Barbara?'

It was Aina, the leader of the union, sitting with her friend Gunda, waiting and hoping to be involved. By the time Fitz came back, all set to work through the night to help me, the job was done. I started to realize that the problem with the so-called rebels was that their energies were being wasted. They were Lithuanian and Latvian and came from the same stock as myself, and all they wanted was to be involved and recognized, and have the chance to prove themselves.

The next day I moved on to the shoe department, a huge mirrored unit right in the middle of the ground floor. We arrived as usual at 8 a.m. and found to our amazement that the stock was already laid out waiting for us. Normally we would spend about an hour waiting for the hands to arrive to enable us to start. To find everything in place when we got there was a miracle. Far away in a corner on our newly installed escalator sat the six committee members of the union, looking rather sheepish. We went over and Fitz thanked them.

'Well,' said Aina, with some contempt, 'she can't do it by herself, can she?'

Not only had they helped but they had helped with thought and understanding. These girls, who had been with us for two or three years, dealing with customers under terrific pressure all day long, really did know what we were trying to do, sometimes more than we realized.

Although the whole inside of the store had been designed eighteen months before, the big unknown factor was the Rainbow Room, with its stage and 500-seat restaurant. The first evening that we finally had the empty store to ourselves Fitz and I went on a grand tour of our new home. The fifth floor, which was entirely given over to the Rainbow Room and its enormous kitchens and subsidiary banqueting rooms, was dark. As we entered the restaurant, gagging slightly on the accumulated cooking smells of fifty years, we sensed something moving in the darkness. Fitz lit a match. The carpet seemed to be moving and suddenly we realised that it was seething with mice, who scurried squeaking and squealing in all directions. It was an incredible sight and it brought home to us just what a dilapidated building we had acquired.

We advertised for a restaurant manager in the catering trade press. The people who applied didn't have anything like the experience that we were looking for, until one of the final applicants arrived with masses of press cuttings praising his work and testifying to his experience in organizing everything from royal banquets to private gourmet evenings. He had even written two books on catering and appeared to be the answer to all our problems. He was short, tubby and French, with a bright red wig and a happy smiling face.

He immediately started to give us a course of instruction on the finer aspects of his art. Every evening he would take us to a restaurant that he thought was particularly suitable to demonstrate a point. After a few weeks we were feeling like stuffed geese but we thought that we were starting to understand what it was all about.

We had chosen the firm of Myton, a subsidiary of the very big Taylor Woodrow group, as overall contractors for the site. It was a very prestigious job for them and they wanted to have an official signing party with photographs being taken for the building trade press. This was obviously an ideal chance for us to test the practical skills of our new catering manager. There were to be about fifty people present for a buffet lunch to be held in Fitz's office and we decided that we would really go overboard to provide the most exotic snacks and canapés that we could think of. The chef was briefed down to the last detail and we set up a temporary kitchen to his specification while the original kitchens were being modernized. We then became involved in other things and thought little about it until the day of the lunch.

The office filled with high-powered dark-suited gentlemen, the drink was going down at a great rate and everybody was happy. A message came from the kitchen that there would be a slight delay before the masterpieces were ready. The signing ceremony came and went and the drinking gathered pace. It was a warm spring day and after about an hour and a half of solid boozing the strain was beginning to tell. Fitz went to the kitchen to hurry things up before our guests were laid out on the carpet. He came back with a stunned look and took me to a corner.

'He's pissed,' Fitz said.

'What about the food?' I asked.

'There's two girls frying sausages on a primus stove,' he replied.

Finally the food arrived, platters of doorstep sandwiches and rolls. They must have been yesterday's, for the outside crust was hard and the rolls were slightly brittle in the middle. They were clamped around enormous sausages – two to each roll. Most of the people in the room were building executives, big men used to big lunches, and all of them were well into their drinks. There were subdued expressions of relief. Fitz was standing talking to the managing director of the entire Myton Group as he took his first bite. As his teeth encountered the stale resistance of the roll his jaws bulged. With a grunt he

burst through the first obstacle. His teeth then met further oppos-
ition and snapped shut on a half-cooked sausage inside. There was a
brief moment while he wrestled to disengage it. Then, the entire rub-
bery sausage was sticking out of his mouth, and – even worse – it had
not been cut from its mate which was dangling beneath it and dripping tomato sauce down his white shirt front. This scene was taking
place all over the room. The orderly if slightly fuddled buzz of conversation was replaced by muted shouts of dismay as immaculate
men stood with drink in one hand, roll in the other and dripping
lumps of half cooked sausage hanging from their mouths. In the
middle of this fiasco, the chef arrived, sweating and triumphant,
toupé askew to receive his applause. The room started to clear as our
guests left hastily before they were subjected to a further course. It
was impossible for us to be angry – we were laughing too much and
the deal was signed – but our quest for a chef who could actually cook
began again the next morning.

During the daytime we were going to split the Rainbow Room into
two sections: a restaurant and two snack bars. We wanted to serve
snacks that were fresh and interesting, bordering on health food. The
first person we asked to be our consultant was Elizabeth David but
she could see that the project was going to be a life's work and
declined. Then I thought of Diana Walsh, who had been cooking for
us on special occasions and keeping our refrigerator stacked with
quiches and pâtés and pies. She and I set to work. Every day she
would arrive at the office loaded with her experiments and we would
test them on the staff, noting their preferences. The snack bar part
was going well, but we were still searching for a restaurant manager.

Finally we met Alan Gearing, a short, rugged Liverpudlian. Fitz
took him up to the restaurant and explained what we were trying to
do. Alan nodded away until Fitz asked him directly, 'Do you know
what you're talking about?'

'Would I mislead you?' said Alan.

'Yes,' said Fitz, and took him on.

Alan brought with him two chefs, also from the north, called Big
John and Little John. Every lunchtime Fitz and I and anyone we
could find would join Alan and his men at a formal table at one end
of the echoing Rainbow Room, and we would all sit solemnly munch-
ing our way through the dishes, approving or rejecting as we ate.

In those days the fashion in food was for it to be smothered in heavy sauces. We wanted a style of cooking that was much simpler, letting the natural flavours do the work. Of course this is far more difficult. The standard of both the ingredients and the cooking has to be far higher when there's no spicy sludge to disguise it.

The only other restaurant we knew of that was as large as the Rainbow Room and that was also open all day and night was La Coupole in Paris. We went there one night and introduced ourselves, very humbly, to the director in charge. We explained what we were doing and he immediately agreed to show us round behind the scenes, to see how his whole operation worked. I think he felt sorry for us. For over a hundred years La Coupole had been *the* meeting place for everybody, and he had just discovered two loonies who had come off the street and wanted to start at the same level overnight. It was a fascinating hour for us, seeing behind the scenes of such a vast, famous restaurant.

In the middle of the confusion at the new shop, Sir Hugh Fraser visited us. He walked round the store with Fitz and found thirty girls scratching labels off multicoloured buckets on the household floor. 'Where did those girls come from?' he asked.

'They're our union,' said Fitz proudly.

Sir Hugh looked at him. 'I could never get my people to do that,' he said, and marched on.

That Christmas, in 1972, we visited India to find factories to produce clothes. Daphne, my cloth assistant, was with us when we reached Bombay. Fitz met the Minister of Export. For the next few days Fitz helped him label a mammoth order for C & A while Daphne and I were let loose in a vast room full of manufacturers' fabric swatches. Any cloth that appeared really new and interesting was always dated 1880. Covered in dust, we came to the conclusion that it was much easier to deal with our agent in London. At the weekend, we hired a car and a driver who had previously chauffeured George Harrison and Patti Boyd on their recent trip to India. He insisted on taking us to all the places which they had visited. One was a temple near Bombay. In the centre of the temple was an enormous fertility symbol. If you walked round it and patted it something would happen. I forbade Fitz and Witold to go anywhere near it, but Daphne kept walking round and patting it. She was married, with a little girl, and the following year she had triplets!

On the last day everything was as nearly ready as we were going to get it. It was a Sunday and all our staff had been working non-stop twelve hours a day for three weeks. Every sweater was in its pigeonhole, every last fireproofed plastic grape was in place on the children's floor, shoes and room sets and men's suits were all in position. The food hall could only do their display at the last minute, for obvious reasons. The security guards were in their uniforms. The waiters had had endless hours of rehearsal.

Fitz called everyone down to the ground floor and talked to them. They were all there, our own staff, and no one else. I sat amongst them, I was one of them. Normally it takes hours to get people together but this time they all assembled at five minutes' notice, eager and exhausted, to hear what was expected of them. As I sat there, I became aware with true clarity for the first time of the emotions that had been unleashed in this enterprise. Everyone had worked hard, without overtime money, and felt proud of it. I felt proud of them, too, and part of an equal community.

I felt almost disappointed that the preparations were over. Fitz and I took a final walk through the six floors and 400,000 square feet of our total empire. I rummaged into stockrooms and staffrooms and offices, but I could find nothing wrong. There were many things I wanted to improve, but basically we were as strong as we would ever be, or could be at that moment.

We left well before midnight. It was the first time we had been outside the Big Biba and could see it with all the lights blazing in the windows. I knew that it was not perfect, but I thought I had a lifetime to make it so.

Chapter Nine

At about 4 o'clock in the morning Fitz woke me. We washed quickly and sat for a few minutes drinking coffee, gearing ourselves up for the day ahead. I was feeling absolutely drained. My work was finished the moment those doors opened and the public came in. For the past two years I had thought of little but this day and now it had arrived. I was oddly calm. Fitz, on the other hand, was crazed with energy. To him his job was just starting. He had calculated and budgeted the sales of every item in every department and he couldn't wait to find out what would really happen.

We returned to the shop at about six that morning. The first of the cooks were already at work and the security guards were padding through the deserted floors. There was nothing we could do except check the cleaning once again and hope that the sales girls would arrive on time. By 8 o'clock the exhausted manageresses had dragged themselves back in and the first trickle of other staff began. As the opening hour of 9.30 approached Fitz and I did a last check of the floors. Everything was immaculate. Behind each counter and till stood a nervously expectant girl. Manageresses were chasing late-comers out of the staffrooms. We were ready to go.

We went down to the ground floor, where the security guards were waiting to open the door. This was a very special moment not only for us but for many of the staff who had worked with superhuman strength to get us to this day. To our dismay we discovered that we had visitors. The directors of Dorothy Perkins, whom we had not seen for the past year while we were wrestling with the problems of the new store, were all there in their pinstripe suits.

At 9.30 the doors opened, and there was instant pandemonium. Almost immediately the tills were clattering and by the time we had retreated to the fifth floor, five minutes later, there was already a crowd around the snack bar.

Feeling slightly dazed that the store actually *had* opened, we headed for Fitz's office. We were both tired out and wanted a few moments' peace. Seated at Fitz's desk was Roxburgh, in high spirits, heroically explaining on the telephone to the *Financial Times* how he had performed to get the store open. He looked at us as if we were intruders. Leaving him to it, we wandered back to the crowded sales floors.

'He just couldn't wait,' said Fitz.

But we were not to escape that easily from the self-appointed hero of the hour. About an hour later I was on the children's floor, worrying about the sweater stock that seemed to be going down awfully fast, when I was summoned back to Fitz's office, where Roxburgh had made himself thoroughly at home. A waiter had just been diverted from the frantically busy restaurant to supply him with coffee, and two chairs had been placed in front of the desk for Fitz and me. There is something really degrading about having to sit in front of your own desk in your own office listening to someone sitting in your place.

Roxburgh started to expand on his grand theory. Biba was to be 'institutionalized'. I had no idea what he was talking about but as he went on I gathered that this meant that I was to have very little to do in the future. My job was to be somehow, miraculously, split up among a whole committee of nameless people. I couldn't believe my ears. I was being pushed out before anyone had any idea of even the first morning's sales.

Fitz and I were speechless. A clerk put his head round the door and gave Fitz a piece of paper. I knew it would be the sales figure for up to 12.30. Fitz looked at the paper, showed it to me, and then handed it to Roxburgh, who had no way of knowing if the figure was good or bad. Fitz did nothing to enlighten him so in the end he had to ask. Before we open a new shop Fitz always writes down his sales forecasts. The figure was exactly the same as the one he had predicted. Roxburgh looked startled and left shortly afterwards.

After that they seemed to want us to make mistakes, to be wrong, so that they would be able to step in. But as the days passed and Fitz's forecasts were consistently accurate, our pinstriped friends disappeared and we were left in peace for a time. We knew they would be back.

While optimism was still high I felt we could win any war by just willing the baddies away. We had many happy times in the Big Biba. Few were aware of the battles that were fought in the boardroom.

We were going to open the Roof Garden to the public in the spring of 1974. I was very nervous as we had already heard rumours that locals, old ladies, thought we were going to ruin it by pulling out the trees and replacing them with tennis courts. Fitz was interviewed on radio by Simon Jenkins, the conservationist, and he assured him that if anything we had restored it as we had restored the rest of the building.

The trees on the roof were in a very bad way and we had to call in a tree surgeon to inspect them. He said most would only last one more year. That first and last spring/summer we planted trees, shrubs and flowers with endless energy. Every bare piece of earth was filled with seedlings and sproutings. My theory was that if there was enough seed in the soil something would have to come out to its full glory.

Every evening after work the new-founded gardening club, which consisted of Del, Daphne and Eva clad in sequined jerkins and glitter wellies, and Pam Brown of the baby department, would set out for the roof armed with a tray of Pimms. The gardens in front of the roof restaurant were to be filled with English country flowers. It was going to look like a page from a Kate Greenaway book, so hollyhocks, lupins, daisies, cornflowers and pansies were planted at random. Through the garden a stream flowed, awaiting the arrival of the pink flamingoes. The Spanish garden at the back would be more kitsch. We would fill the beds with peach geraniums, pink peonies and giant blue delphiniums.

During our feverish planting Justin de Villeneuve arrived with a friend. He introduced him as Tony. As I said hello, quite calmly I think, I was in my seventh heaven – Justin and I were having tea with Tony Curtis.

The Tudor Garden was left for Andrew Logan to sculpture his giant roses and devise a black and white garden with a giant white lily as a centrepiece. Andrew spent months casting his masterpiece. He dedicated the two giant sculptured roses to Fitz and me. The centre of the Tudor Garden was going to be a pool out of which grew gigantic irises, with water spouting like a fountain. Their roots seemed to spout water as well. The area below the pool was the restaurant kitchen. Right under Andrew's pool, the sandwiches were continually soaked by his fountain. Andrew wanted to dedicate the next black rose to Witold. It would grow over the top of the building and be suspended over the High Street. With even our energy flagging, the thought of trying to convince the local council of the feasibility of this proved too much for either of us. We had enough trouble from all directions without a gigantic black rose landing on somebody's head below. I was beginning to feel the spookiness that black evokes. On the flagpoles flew black banners. Black is an evil colour and provokes the Devil. It is very unlucky if you don't pay court to him.

We waited the arrival of the flamingoes and the penguins with some anxiety. We had rented them from Billy Smart, who would advise us and look after the birds if they got ill. The flamingoes arrived in a long wooden crate. We all rushed up to the Roof Garden to watch them unpacked. Inside the box each flamingo was packed in a nylon stocking. They lay there grotesquely, head to foot, like giant rhubarb sticks.

After the flamingoes were settled in the penguins arrived. They were magnificent. They looked perfect in Andrew's black and white garden, but they preferred the pond past the Billy Goats Gruff bridge. When the twelve penguins were allowed out of their boxes they went in a band to investigate the pond. They had a little swim but were not very impressed. Their leader decided to see if he might find better quarters. He or she waddled off, followed by the others, towards the back staircase that led into the Rainbow Room. Although we were in stitches from laughing, we had been warned not to go too near them as they could be vicious. So the penguins continued down the stairs in single file into the Rainbow Room. We had to summon the security guard to try and redirect them back on to the roof. Half an hour later the penguin general returned to the Roof Garden followed by the other penguins, which in turn were followed by the entire security force. We were all sad when they had to be sent back. The water in the pond was too muddy for them and they just stood in huddles on the bank and shivered. Penguins like cold crystal clear waters.

The opening party of the Roof Garden was spectacular. Everyone drank a bright green crème de menthe cocktail which looked innocuous but turned out to be lethal. Aina and Gunda arrived dressed in funereal black, black gloves and black veils thrown over their black, wide brimmed hats. They sat in silence drinking the emerald liquid through straws under their veils. I was a bit worried as Prudence Glynn of *The Times* was sitting near them. Aina and Gunda were too far gone to notice anybody.

There were fire-eaters, and a prim string trio under the monkey puzzle tree playing Bach and Vivaldi. The tightrope walker in the Tudor Garden fell off her rope and got stabbed by one of Andrew's irises. The contortionist was suspended over the High Street by his feet. The Spanish Garden was full of children, shrieking and paddling in the Moorish fountains. Andrew's brother roller skated around the gardens. Sweetalk sang beautiful songs. The day ended at midnight when Lindsay Kemp did a dance round the iris-filled pool.

The following morning the gardens were opened to the public. We took a fortune in two-shilling pieces. The old ladies were out in full force. I sat on a bench listening to their remarks. We were in – they approved. We had not ruined their beautiful garden. They even liked the children's area filled with gnomes and bambis and fibreglass toadstool tables and chairs.

My friends came to visit us from across the ocean when the Roof Garden was open. Marcia Israel arrived one day and I thought Molly Parkin, then in her emerald green period, would shock and amuse her. Throughout that lunch Marcia pretended not to notice Molly's bright green hair.

A few months after the opening the Wombles launched their new record on the Roof Garden. At the same time Witold held his seventh birthday party. Witold's nanny made a date with a Womble but he stood her up. One Womble was fascinated by shopkeeping and grilled me for hours about turnovers and stock levels. I couldn't keep a straight face throughout this conversation with a woolly animal. Nothing could mar that magical afternoon, even though my eight-year-old niece asked me what was going to happen to the straw peacock chairs when Biba closed. There must have been some wishful thinking in her home.

There was one hair-raising week at teatime. We only had fifty cups left. Our black china took longer to make than the ordinary kind and for the next week it was touch and go whether the cups could be washed up in time to serve the flow of customers. It's one of the problems of having a restaurant, the fact that you can never enjoy or relax. You are forever worrying about what horrors will happen next when somebody especially important is being entertained.

One floor down from the Roof Garden was the Rainbow Room, named after the huge oval Art Deco ceiling that could be illuminated from within with an almost endless permutation of colours. The room was vast, over 10,000 square feet. We had covered the central dining area in pink marble and for the surrounds we had a specially woven copy of the original carpet. One entire side was taken up by a huge bar, supervised by Jimmy, an Irishman with some repute as a hurley player. On the other side were the snack bars, one for food and one for soft drinks and ice cream. At one end was a stage and at the other end the beautiful doors of the lifts. It looked like a film set. In the daytime Fitz and I were too busy to pay it much attention, but at night, as the shop closed, we would meet on the fifth floor and a new set of problems would beset us.

Outside Fitz's office there was an ante-room with desks in it where his secretary and a couple of people who worked in the Rainbow Room made their office. On the first visit of the pinstripe brigade from Dorothy Perkins one of the lads was powdering his nose with cocaine. Being unaware of such goings on the pinstripe brigade passed him by without another look. I was told by a friend that sort of thing could make trouble and I should let Fitz know. Since I was as green as the pinstripe brigade this coke-snorting business was as much of a surprise to me as it was when someone told us about our two spaced out guards in Church Street.

In general the people who work in the catering business are very happy-go-lucky. We had some great people working for us. Apart from Alan Gearing, the manager, and the two Johns, there was Tony, a tall West Indian cook who had worked for the Rolling Stones; Bruce, the Swiss pastry chef from the Dorchester; Eddie Hunt, who was in charge of the groups and musicians; Diana and Anthea, who ran the snack bar, assorted waiters, waitresses and kitchen hands – a total staff of over 150 people. The pressures on them were enormous. We were open from 9.30 a.m. until two the next morning and we were serving over two thousand meals a day.

Despite the training that everyone had been given in the weeks before the store opened, the first night was a near disaster. The restaurant seated over six hundred and it appeared to us as if everybody from both the press and the catering business were there to watch us fall flat on our faces.

On one of our trips to America we had come upon a truly remarkable singer called Sandy Ames in a restaurant in Sarasota on the Gulf of Mexico. She had the saddest and most lovely voice I'd ever heard. It could have belonged to a torch singer in a Humphrey Bogart film. We employed her on the spot although I don't think she really believed that we were serious. When she finally arrived, months later, I was starting to doubt my judgement and rushed her to the piano where the manageresses and union committee were sitting waiting to hear her. When she started playing and singing everyone just melted. She was perfect.

To make sure that the restaurant was running smoothly on the first night we had planted some of our friends among the customers to report back to us if things seemed to be going wrong. Fitz and I were charging back and forth between the kitchen and the reception desk. Sandy Ames came on for her first performance and was given rapturous applause, so we started to relax. In our concern about the food we hadn't been paying much attention to the waiters. One of our friends came up to us and whispered, 'No one is being served'. There should have been over forty waiters on the floor and there was not one in sight. Unbelievable, but they were all having their own supper. We found them in the staff restaurant happily eating away, head waiters and all.

After many fights with Alan and the two Johns about serving fresh peas, I had won. We would serve only fresh vegetables. But the day Fay Maschler, the restaurant critic for the *Evening Standard*, wrote a damning article on our cooking, referring to our frozen peas, I gave in to the chefs. If people couldn't tell the difference it wasn't worth it.

The first live group that we booked were the New York Dolls. They had a big following in Manhattan, where their fans had recently wrecked the ballroom at the Waldorf Astoria. It was their first visit to England and we thought we were lucky to get them. The day that they were due to appear we were watching their roadies setting up the equipment when the head of our security arrived, gripping two bedraggled looking creatures who had been caught shoplifting dresses and who claimed to work for us. They were part of the group and reluctantly we had to let them off. The Dolls did not go down very well with our audience, either.

Through the connections of Eddie Hunt and Alan Gearing we quickly became a special place where overseas groups could perform before a highly appreciative audience as a showcase for the critics and record company producers, before embarking on tours. Among the groups and artists to appear were Bill Haley and his Comets, Jimmy Cliff, the Drifters, the Pointer Sisters, George Melly, Manhattan Transfer, the Kinks, and Procul Harum. At the same time we ran a regular Friday night show with groups that had yet to be discovered. Eddie Hunt was marvellous at spotting the up and coming stars just before they became big. We had the Bay City Rollers, Cockney Rebel and the Average White Band, all within weeks of their first hit records.

A particular favourite of ours was Tim Hardin. We had met him through Justin de Villeneuve, who was his manager in the early 1970s. Tim was making one of his comebacks after falling asleep on the stage during a solo performance at the Albert Hall, which had not endeared him to the promoters. Justin had cured this unfortunate habit by standing in the wings with a pea shooter. Every time Tim seemed to be losing concentration he would let him have a sharp one behind the ear. On this occasion it really worked. Only those in the know could notice the occasional jerk from Tim as Justin reminded him of what he was meant to be doing. At the end of the show Tim Hardin had a standing ovation from the admittedly invited crowd from the recording industry. Unhappily he blew the whole thing immediately afterwards when he rushed up to Fitz and in front of the cream of the recording business told us, with blazing eyes, how he had taught those arseholes a lesson. Another one of our regular groups was Kilburn and the High Roads, managed by Tommy Roberts of Mr Freedom fame.

The Liberace Fan Club had booked the Rainbow Room for their banquet to coincide with the maestro's visit to London to launch his book. This was an evening I couldn't miss. I hung around in a corner by the lifts waiting for his arrival. We had instructions from the president of the fan club how she wished the tables to be arranged and the piano had to be set up amongst them. I felt a small contribution from Biba would be to supply a candelabra, although there had been no mention of the most important prop. Del went down to Sotheby's to hire the biggest and most spectacular one she could find.

She returned with a bronze eighteenth-century six-candled rococo monster dripping with crystal. It was valued at £4,000 and had to be brought back the next day. We placed the bronze monster on the white grand piano. It looked out of place but what the hell? Half an hour before Mr Liberace's planned arrival the three lifts opened and the generals of the fan club marched into the Rainbow Room. Their uniform was black dresses, strings of pearls and platinum mink stoles. Each general carried Georgian silver candelabras and other silver table ornaments. They stormed into action, banishing our bronze monster to the other end of the room. Looking defiant and rather out of place, our candelabra stood sparkling on a fake Art Deco reception desk.

This was going to be a very heavy evening, or at least I thought it was. On the dot of eight the telephone rang with a message from security saying that Mr Liberace was on his way up.

The doors slid open and the lovely fresh-faced, sparkling Liberace sailed into the Rainbow Room. He looked magnificent in his white mink double-breasted coat fastened by rows of real diamond buttons. What puzzled me was that right behind me were Andrew Logan and Zandra Rhodes wearing a Sheherezade turban. I wandered over to Andrew and Zandra and asked them how on earth they'd got invitations. They replied that they hadn't. They were just gatecrashing, but with such panache! They were both armed with Instamatic cameras and Andrew was clutching a bread roll. Before the evening was out he had got Liberace's autograph on his tie *and* on the roll.

I really wanted to meet Liberace. Suddenly he was by my side, saying hello. We chatted away. He adored the store, particularly the leopard skin luggage, and couldn't wait to come in the next morning to do some shopping. His admiring gaze was fixed on the bronze candelabra. I felt a stab in my shin from Joyce, our hostess. I could see that any moment I might feel obliged to present him with our hired prop. I had instructed Joyce to kick me hard if she saw I was about to give it to him as a memento of his evening in Biba. I pulled round, and Sotheby's got their great candelabra back the next day.

Molly Parkin was now in her red and white period. All her clothes were unfailingly in these colours. On the launch of her first book her publishers threw a party for her in Fitz's enormous office, which had been a small banqueting room. I asked Alan Gearing to prepare a feast.

Everything edible was to be red and white. Alan and I let rip. We decided to make all the savoury things look like cakes. As a centrepiece the pastrycook made a mashed potato cake elaborately decorated as if it was a white cream cake with beetroot roses. At this party Molly introduced me to her newest discovery – Regis the visagiste.

We were going to open a beauty parlour on the third floor. We had been looking for someone who could take charge of the hairdressing and, most important of all, the make-up, so that you could go in and have your hair and face made up in beautiful surroundings, and be truly transformed for the evening ahead. When Regis took the department over one of his first customers was Britt Ekland, who came for a bit of improvement before the première of the James Bond film in which she starred. Regis made her look amazing. Her hair looked like a lion's mane and her make-up was superb. When she made the grand entrance at the première nobody recognized her. The photographers thought she was merely a stunning model, and ignored her.

Before each do at the Rainbow, Regis would transform Joyce and the other hostesses into magnificent vamps, who would often outshine all the customers. Unfortunately I never had time to lounge in the hairdresser's or maybe I never had the patience to sit for hours looking at my own awful reflection. The only time I have ever been to a hairdresser was to Leslie at Leonard, who is now an owner of Smile, who did Cathy McGowan's hair. He was the only person who understood people with straight hair who hide behind a fringe. My hairstyle comes into fashion every ten years but there is one consolation – when it does I am one of the first to be wearing it!

After Regis came, the only things we lacked in Biba were a funeral parlour and a cinema!

We were constantly asked to organize exhibitions and promotions for other people, but usually their products or ideas were out of keeping with what we were trying to do. One that we were very glad to accept was an exhibition of the work of handicapped children, another was the launch of the *Rock Dreams* book by Nik Cohn and Guy Pallaert. We also launched a Marilyn Monroe exhibition to coincide with the book by Norman Mailer, with a mass of memorabilia including the original nude calendar.

Perhaps our *pièce de résistance* was the New Year's Eve party of 1973.

Andrew Logan had just started his Alternative Miss World Competition. I had met him a few years before, when Biba was part of the Cecil Beaton Exhibition at the Victoria and Albert Museum, and he had become a friend. The central part of the evening was to be a fancy dress competition organized and judged by Andrew and his friends. As midnight approached, Mynah Bird, a well-known lady about town, was to leap out of a huge cake carried by four professional strong men. Aina had taped Big Ben at midnight and was responsible for playing it at the right time. There was a net full of balloons to be released and the Rainbow Room was packed out. Our personal guests were a good cross section of our friends: Molly Parkin and her then husband Patrick Hughes, the painter, Robert Lacey, the author, and his wife Sandy, John Kobal, the film historian, our Italian friends Nally and Manfredi Bellati, Janet Street-Porter and Tim, her ex-husband, Felicity Green and her husband Geoffrey Hill, Liz and David Smith, Tony Elliott, the publisher of *Time Out*, and Michael Roberts of the *Sunday Times*, who was dressed as Diana Ross.

The evening was a riot. Fitz was introduced by Del to the strongmen that she had hired to lift the cake. Four enormous and polite men, immaculately dressed in dark suits, shook him gravely by the hand and asked if it was all right to bring in their wives and girlfriends. Fitz thought they looked familiar. When he saw them stripped for action in the leopard loincloths we had had made for them, he realized that Del had unknowingly hired the cream of professional wrestlers, headed by the great Tibor Sackas.

'Christ!' said Fitz. 'Thank heavens I was nice to them.'

We had built a catwalk several feet off the ground, which ran for 20 yards up the middle of the room. By the time the contest started, at about ten, many of the predominantly male entrants, dressed in the most exotic evening clothes, had become remarkably drunk. The catwalk was a challenge that several failed to beat. I will never forget one sedate couple, who had secured a prize seat beside the catwalk, gazing in stunned disbelief at a hairy male bottom emerging from a white dress whose owner had collapsed, stomach first, across their table. They were still there three hours later, so they must have been enjoying themselves. The din that night was incredible. At about 12.15 I sensed that something was wrong. Everybody was waiting for 'Auld Lang Syne', but there was no Big Ben. I went backstage to find Aina struggling with the recorder. When she finally got it going, at about 12.30, it started in the middle of the reel but nobody seemed to notice. As the bells sounded we released the net full of balloons. Somehow we had not got it quite right; the balloons came down all right, but when the waiters in charge tried to raise the net several customers had become attached to it and were dangling above the heads of the rest of the crowd, who grandly ignored them. We released the net and let the hanging guests crash back into the crowd.

This was easier said than done. The problems of communication with over a thousand drunken revellers in a room are hard to overcome. At each corner of the net were two waiters who thought they were supposed to pull up the net. Fitz was frantically signalling to them to stop, but the more he waved the more they pulled, eyes bulging with the unexpected effort of lifting the bodies. Alan Gearing ran up to Fitz through the demented crowd.

'They'll be bloody dying soon!' he shouted.

He and Fitz charged through the milling bodies and wrested the ropes from the waiters. The net and its contents disappeared into the mass. Nobody seemed to bother and there were no dead bodies in the morning. All this may bear out the theory that you can take a fall without pain or fracture if you're drunk, but I think that we were very lucky.

The wrestlers made their ceremonious entrance carrying the cake. Mynah Bird, who had been crouched inside for quite a while, leaped out at the wrong cue and was left standing solemnly on the catwalk in her pink bikini as Andrew Logan announced the prize winners.

At the other end of the scale, our banqueting business was growing. Our most notable occasion was the Butterfly Ball. It was the most glittering charity occasion of the year, and was to be graced by Princess Margaret. The organizer was Lady Jane Wellesley, and her brother Lord Douro was one of the main sponsors. In the end it turned out to be a most successful evening but it was somewhat soured for me by what seemed really carping protocol from the Palace. One of the royal aides had visited the building and decided that the Princess needed her own rest room and private loo. The only suitable place that could be found was Fitz's office, which had its own loo complete with the most marvellous 1930s French *pissoir*. This would absolutely not do. Our carpenters wasted a whole day boxing in this architectural marvel. I had never encountered anything so silly. At a crazy time of our lives the Rainbow Room in a funny way helped us to keep our sense of perspective and sanity.

Chapter Ten

It has always been a joke between Fitz and me that in this country the creative decisions are usually made by the managing director's wife. She is to blame for the 'creative' output in industry. She has designed and instigated cigarette packs and graphic swirls around the saucepans while the art schools have been belching out hoards of talented people who fall by the wayside as there are not enough design jobs. In England a designer in any form is still a dangerous animal to be touched only with a poker. No money is spent on experiments. The cost of a designer is a minute percentage of the rewards. But designers who become powerful because of their success are a very dangerous force to any big company. They can always walk away with their talents. So the theory is that it's better to be mediocre and safe than very good and in the power of that 'beast'. The only way for the 'beast' to flourish is to have his own business.

I have noticed over the years that men have frequently become unsettled at the relationship between Fitz and me. They either try to shoulder Fitz out or they start to involve their own wives in things that are strictly our business. As soon as a wife appears on the scene, I smell trouble. After Big Biba had opened and the dirty work was over, ladies who had spent the last nine years having children and going to the hairdresser, while I had been working flat out, suddenly became experts whose opinion was sought, whose 'woman's view' was courted, and whose preferences I was meant to listen to. The opinion of the directors' wives was of no interest to me. In my view, their only claim to importance was their husband's position.

Our relationship with our fellow directors soon received another jolt. One morning we received an invitation to a dinner party at No.10 Downing Street. We had been there once before, but our instant reaction was that it was a hoax. Feeling rather foolish, Fitz rang the number on the invitation, only to be assured that it was genuine. When our co-directors heard about it I thought they would have apoplexy. Edward Heath was then prime minister and the dinner was in honour of the visiting prime minister of Japan. Our previous visit to Downing Street had been in the days of Harold Wilson, and we had been part of a whole mob who had been gathered together to greet a rather bewildered Willy Brandt. It had been one of Mr Wilson's famous Swinging Sixties' salons which, he claimed, put the White House parties in the shade. We were all herded into two huge rooms and, although the champagne kept on coming, nobody knew anyone else and we all stood around rather awkwardly watching Sandie Shaw in her stockinged feet posing with the great man. Most people left as early as they decently could.

This time it was quite different. About fifty people, most of them diplomats and their wives, had been invited to a sit-down dinner. We were staggered to find that all these grand ladies were Biba regulars. They seemed to know more about our store than we did. Mr Heath had obviously done his homework, for when he introduced me to the Japanese party he gave them a brief and very complimentary description of our career. It was a lovely evening. My overall impression was of immense politeness and friendliness – we felt shy at first but were made to feel at ease.

For the first six weeks everything ran like clockwork. All the departments were selling over their forecast figures, new stock was flowing in, and we were starting to relax. Then came the miners' strike and the start of the three-day working week of early 1974. At the same time the property market collapsed. Biba's sales, along with everyone else's, were badly hit and suddenly the complaints started to come pouring in. It seemed that every time Mr Ritblat went on a social visit he would meet somebody who had something detrimental to say or a suggestion to make. One minute we had been hailed as geniuses, and the next our staff could do nothing right.

It was obvious to us both that we were entering the final stages of the battle. These started with a sudden barrage of internal memos. One that had everyone in stitches was about menstruation and absence of leave. All female staff were allowed one day off per month, but by some administrative folly the memo had been sent to both male and female staff!

Underground literature started to appear in lavatories, staff rest rooms and the canteen. The pinstripe brigade became very worried and excited when a poem derogatory to Mr Ritblat was pushed into the sanctum of their Think Tank. An official pinstripe delegation came to see Fitz early the next morning. They were fuming and obviously terrified of his reaction. They wanted to make an example of someone. This little prank was a criminal attack on the reputation of a great man. They suspected that the heart of this scurrilous rebellion was in our press room, now being manned by our trade union committee. They were going straight down there to secure the evidence and then they would call the police. It was madness.

Fitz and I had seen the defamatory leaflet the previous day. We thought it was guaranteed to stir things up and I was eager to illustrate it but Fitz said that my drawings would be too easy to identify so I dropped that idea. As the seething little knot of men stormed out of his office, Fitz called the press room and spoke to Aina, the chairwoman of the union. By the time the delegation arrived the entire union committee was waiting for them. All the evidence, including one masterly 'British Land is Underhand' slogan, had magically disappeared and the Perkers left, grinding their teeth. Later on the same girls, Aina, Gunda, Joyce and Lily, were planning to chain themselves to the railings outside the hotel where the British Land annual general meeting was taking place. Fortunately it was a freezing day and we managed to dissuade them. It was important that the battle did not turn into a farce.

The daily cleaning of the building was a nightmare. It took almost a week to scrub one well of the backstairs. By the time the cleaner had got to the top, the bottom upwards was filthy again and littered with empty cans of drinks and screwed up papers. Once one well was finished, the other one which led to the kitchens had to be attacked. Unless you checked up on its daily progress the cleaner would disappear. Our great dread was that one day we would come in early in the morning to find the ground floor untouched. However many wastepaper bins there were, the floor was always littered with papers, cans and plain old muck by the end of each day. The strong light from the windows showed up all the marks on the marble. We had chosen hard flooring as it was by far the easiest to look after. Lino was hell to scrub clean and if done badly looked even worse. Carpet, however tough, just wore to bare patches in a matter of weeks. I felt my destiny was going to be an eternal housekeeper, like Mrs Danvers in *Rebecca*. It was like the Forth Bridge – just as they finish painting it the time is right to start again. Now it makes me feel exhausted just to think of the cleaning problems. The fun really came when there was a downpour. No one knew where the floods would appear. Logically you would think it was the top floor which would be affected, but in that building it was the fourth floor where the buckets would have to come out.

Neither did we realize what obstacles to communication the size of the building would present. Firstly, to try and find anybody was a nightmare. If you took a lift up to look for someone you could bet your bottom dollar they had just taken another lift down. The only thing to do was to issue all management with walkie talkies. Not being able even to use an adding machine, this little monster gave me great trouble. It would start bleeping you and it would go on until you talked to it. I could never remember which button to push to silence it. If I popped out to Lyon's next door it would start squealing as I was waiting in the queue for a bun.

By Christmas 1974, things were starting to look up again. The sales returned to their proper level and we were catching up on the ground lost during the strike, but the outside pressures did not let up. By now British Land was in serious difficulties. It is well known that when a company is in trouble, the bosses become obsessively careful with little things like the petty cash. We seemed to be regarded as British Land's petty cash. Although our sales were back on target, the temporary recession had enabled them to establish a beachhead into our business and there was no getting them out.

We were unprepared for what was to come. For the past five years there had been nothing but harmony between us and Dorothy Perkins. Board meetings were only held when it was a legal requirement. Suddenly we were into scoring points. Board meeting after board meeting, following meetings prior to a board meeting when Roxburgh would show his draft of the minutes of the coming meeting to Fitz as they had been anticipated by him. At crucial meetings we were outvoted as we now only had a 25 per cent holding. I was barraged with internal memos. For the last eight years it had never been necessary to write a memo to anyone. With good verbal communication and trust, you didn't need proof that you had instructed someone to do a specific thing. I suddenly had to have a secretary in order to answer their requests. With all these letters toing and froing, our energies were wasted before any real action. But it made them happy: everything down on paper, neatly filed, and that was important to them.

Their tactics would have been acceptable if they had worked better. They introduced what could only be called an alternative administration. One day our own managers found that each of them had a duplicate with the same title doing the same job. It was a shambles – no one knew who was giving orders to whom. The first new person they hired was a large man who looked as if he had started his career as a dummy in the window. Witold came running to me one day, full of excitement, because he had just seen Captain Scarlet, a television puppet hero, walking through the stockroom. This gentleman became Captain Scarlet from that moment on.

For the first time things were starting to go wrong with Witold. Poor little chap, we always assumed he wasn't listening to our conversations which were nothing but problems and worries. As we drove down the High Street one day he suddenly shot up in his seat and cried, 'Give me a Perker – I'll punch them!' We were at that point passing a Dorothy Perkins shop. Often he was sent home from school with a blinding migraine. He would vomit and then sleep as if he was dead for hours.

We were getting very worried about him and our doctor sent us to a paediatrician in Harley Street, who examined him and asked us quite loudly in front of him if we were in the habit of discussing our problems when he was around. Yes, we were, we always included him in everything we did. But the doctor explained that he was much too young to cope with our problems. After that we were very careful what was said in front of him and he rarely developed a migraine again.

With Captain Scarlet as general manager, the Perkers then moved in in earnest; the board found themselves an office and set up what they called a Think Tank. They moved en masse, bringing with them a few of their employees who obviously didn't have much to do where they were. They were not retailers – none of them had ever run a shop in his life. Roxburgh was an accountant, Nichols, the personnel manager, had come up through the wages department, Hammond Turner came from an advertising agency, Collard was yet another accountant, Woodhams was head of Dorothy Perkins's security, and

Mike Davies, a junior manager, was beside himself in his new position. I found he had rearranged the record counter, where there was a sign that said 'American Groups', and changed it himself in pen to 'Groovy'. I had to laugh, but really this was Carnaby Street thinking – not Biba.

Othello's tummy – or the life-sized model of it that we had used – was no longer to be used as a container for pet food. A memo arrived declaring that his statue with its recess for tins was now obsolete and in future all dog food, cat food and fish food was to be displayed on a table covered by a grotty piece of felt.

In desperation Fitz and I asked for a meeting with Ritblat. We tried to present a well-reasoned case and listen to his side, but at one stage I thought that Fitz was going to break his neck. In order to humour him we said that we would go along with his suggestions. We agreed that there was not enough information to the public in the shop. We had done what we thought was correct up to now and the practical necessities only emerged after the shop was reopened. We would follow all John Ritblat's suggestions, stressing that we'd do everything in an organized way. We would have 'Pay Here' signs and 'Cash Desk' signs, but we wanted these done in a way that was right for the feel of the shop. To me it meant we could introduce neon all over the store, which had not been used since the fifties, and I quite liked the idea. It was all agreed at the meeting, but it seemed we were not to be allowed much involvement. Next day a lorry arrived full of Tesco-like white light boxes to be put up all over the store. I was at least allowed to choose the graphics that the signwriter was to paint on them. Their words were 'Groovy Food Hall – arrow – Basement'; 'Cafeteria Self Service Fifth Floor'; 'Maternity', which had formerly been 'Pregnant Mum'; and 'Lolita' was now to be 'Junior Miss'. God, I felt sick. Very early in the morning before anyone arrived I went and jumped up and down on the whole lot. There wasn't one bit of usable white plastic left. I hid it all under the long table that stood in the centre of my office, covered by a cloth. It took security three months to find the debris.

We had never needed any window display. People knew us well enough to understand the mixture of tramps, ladies from the suburbs, the odd priest, and office girls eating their lunch or generally lolling on the seats of the jumbo windows. These spoke more loudly for Biba than any display of stiff dummies would. Did the public need to be reassured by pretentious fibreglass figures in contortionist poses that gleamed false smiles at them to lure them into the store? We thought not, but the Perkers disagreed.

There was no need to talk down to the public. The henchmen had no nous. I was not going to be a part of all this, but I was vital to them as a scapegoat. If their plan didn't work it would be me who was responsible. I received a letter from a girl who had worked for us and had left under a cloud. She said she was not an admirer of Biba now but she knew in her heart of hearts that we *couldn't* be responsible for the shifty-looking shop Biba was fast becoming. That letter gave me confidence to keep fighting. It became my habit to go in very early in the mornings, as I knew they would be up to something. Once I arrived and workmen had ripped out two units on the first floor and were looking lost, wondering what to do next. There were two gaping holes in the marble floor with computer cables and knots of electrical wires staring at them. If they had asked me I would have told them there was no marble under the counters, but the counters were moved to another spot and the gaping holes were left unattended. They had just done as they were told and that was it as far as they were concerned.

Another morning I found workmen sawing away at shelves covered with mirrors. I couldn't work out why they needed to do that, but an order had come from Ritblat to do something about the lighting. Instead of adding more spots to the existing rails, they swivelled all the lamp holders towards the ceiling throwing the whole floor into a grey fog. When the girls arrived in the morning they automatically stretched up with brooms and directed the lighting towards the clothes. But now I wasn't allowed to talk to the staff and was told that the whole store was going to be flooded with strip lighting. This is effective if the level is quite low but on a very high ceiling it becomes very flat and it alters certain colours. My knowledge and experience were just wasted though.

By now I had been defeated on the ground floor. Every inch of spare marble was now covered by supermarket-like units and dump bins. You couldn't move without bumping into something. The sweaters were now à la Marks and Spencer, untouchably sealed in polythene bags. They were so untouchable that customers did not go near them.

Captain Scarlet was put in charge of the Roof Garden. He was going to put his fairy touch on it and transform it into a Japanese theme. Our lovely hollyhocks, lupins and other Kate Greenaway flowers were excavated and red geraniums and yellow chrysanths took their place, but he approved of the kitsch flamingoes. The 'Delphic Grotto' was now to take the place of the carp pond. In happier days the garden had been surrounded by michaelmas daisies. Rumour had it blue plastic chrysanths were about to be implanted instead.

I was now banned from entering the store or talking to any staff but my own lot in the office. I talked to the girls in sign language or by passing notes. It was becoming ludicrous. We had no respect for the British Land mouthpieces, because it was quite clear that they didn't have any conviction about what they were doing. They were just yes men taking orders from above. They treated women like shit and that got up everybody's nose, especially as all the floor staff were female. One day one of our prettiest girls had disappeared. I asked the manageress what had happened. Had she left? She said Mr Roxburgh didn't like the girl's looks so she had been sacked.

Upstairs in the Rainbow Room the glossy black cups and saucers were replaced by paper cups, which then littered the Deco carpets. There was no one to see that they were removed during the day. Nobody cared any more. The public was walking out with lamps, tables and ashtrays. I met a man by the Kensington Odeon carrying a pink mirror coffee table from the Rainbow Room. His partner followed, carrying a lamp under her arm.

It was time for me to go. I couldn't watch the destruction of that beautiful building. It was dreadful to feel so powerless. They could have it. As my parting gesture I ordered five thousand fluorescent plastic buckets for the use of the ground floor. Let them work that one out, I thought.

The irony of the situation is that today the tables have turned. The things that I was fighting for are now accepted. Perhaps I would now be fighting for the wire baskets and strip lighting while they could be trying to lay brown carpets and put in kitsch pink mirrors.

Before I finally made the break and left for good, one evening I went home alone. I was raging with fury. I had to hurt something and the nearest thing was me. I poured every drop of leftover liquor into a jug. There was whisky, Cointreau, vodka, gin and brandy. I shook it all up and drank the cocktail. I still couldn't simmer down. I found my sleeping pills and swallowed the lot. The next thing I knew I was lying in St Mary Abbots Hospital. I heard a voice in my ear, 'Mrs Fitz-Simon, if you don't stop swearing we will have to put you out on the pavement. Can't you tell us what's wrong?' Fitz had come home and found me vomiting my vile cocktail and called an ambulance. I was shocked at myself. If I didn't get a grip on things I would end up in a lunatic asylum and that would be one up for Roxburgh.

Against my better judgement I was inveigled into one last meeting with the entire Dorothy Perkins board. What were they trying to do? Why couldn't they let me go? Roxburgh waved my contract in my face. We had two more years to go and after that we couldn't open a shop within 50 miles of London. He seemed to me to gain pleasure in reminding me of this. I felt claustrophobic and left the building in my Mini. On the way out I got a bottle of gin. I took a swig. By the time I had finished three-quarters of the bottle I had reached the country or at least I thought I had. Maybe it was just a common. It was now dark, I was paralytically drunk and I didn't have the foggiest idea where I was. I stopped by a telephone box. There wasn't a house in sight. I stumbled to the box and dialled Fitz. The instant I finished dialling he answered.

'Where are you?'

I couldn't tell him since I didn't know. He was getting frantic. Suddenly out of the trees came a gang of leather-clad youths. I thought I could see chains in their hands.

'Oh Fitz, they're going to kill me,' I said, and I put the receiver down as they approached. My drunken instinct told me I would be better off being beaten up in the open air than inside. If they had intended to punch me up they soon changed their minds. As I opened the door of the booth, the stink of alcohol must have been appalling. I swayed and looked them straight in the eye. I can't remember how I got home, but the next morning the car was there and so was frantic Fitz.

All this time Fitz had been trying to raise finance to buy our business back. We couldn't have picked a worse time than the mid-seventies, with rising inflation. Most of the merchant banks had been pinched by the collapse of the property market, and London was full of ex-millionaires and people who knew Arabs. The deal Fitz was offering was simple. He had a shrewd idea that British Land's real interest was to sell the building, leaving Biba as tenant. Our first year's sales, despite the three-day week and the beginning of the management meddling, were extremely good. We had said we would take £5 million in the first year and we were only just below that. It was easy to demonstrate that with us in control, Biba was a proposition – none of our would-be partners ever doubted that.

Even now, when people say to me, knowingly, that we bit off more than we could chew, it makes me furious. We knew exactly what we were doing and we did it, and at the time everyone knew that we were right. The end of Biba has been analysed dozens of times, in the financial press and on television, and the reasons are obvious to me.

One of our potential partners was one of the funniest men that Fitz and I have ever met. His name was Ernest Ottewell. He was a property developer from Leicester. He and Fitz were introduced through third parties and immediately became friendly. Although it was a tense and terrible time for us, the fact that we were dealing with someone that we liked made an enormous difference. The problem was that Ernest and Fitz, who were both working on the deal about eighteen hours a day, were such soulmates that things would sometimes tend to get out of hand. Fitz, whose language since his army days had always been fairly fruity, found that Ernest, in the innocent country bumpkin way that he affected when doing a deal, was more than his match. Together they made one of the biggest social gaffes I have ever heard of.

They were talking to a senior partner in a big firm of accountants. One evening a particularly contentious problem had arisen and they were asked round to the accountant's flat in Bayswater to sort it out. The big man was there with his assistant and his wife. Fitz and Ernest, who had passed by a pub on their way, and who were annoyed with the accountant, became extremely heated. While Fitz was going at it hammer and tongs, Ernest in his naive manner was chatting up his wife, making compliments about her beauty and that of her daughters whose pictures were on the wall.

As they drove away, Ernest decided that Fitz had been a bit too strong in front of a lady and when they arrived at our house I heard the tale and agreed with him to send his wife some flowers. I rang his office the next morning, and having discovered his address ordered the flowers and thought no more of it. I sent a note from Fitz apologizing for having disturbed her evening. That poor man! The lady in his flat was his girlfriend and not the mother of the girls in the picture. His real wife, who received the flowers, lived miles out of London and had no idea of the affair, which had been going on for years. Ernest, Fitz and I between us brought his entire world about his ears. He refused ever to have anything to do with any of us again. Who could blame him?

We came so close to doing a deal with British Land that after several weeks of hard negotiation Fitz set off late one afternoon for the final meeting when the contracts would be signed. There were several solicitors and other experts in the room and at literally the last moment a technicality arose that made the deal impossible. When Fitz returned that night we knew that time was running out. Fitz carried on for a while but I bowed out after it was clear that we couldn't regain control and left the store in the hands of British Land.

Although I revelled in their failures, I wanted to cry about what they were doing. Captain Scarlet's first purchase was a lot of funny looking dresses which he displayed in the windows. At the same time, C & A's windows opposite were full of the same styles from the same manufacturer but at half the price. A while after Biba closed British Land sold Dorothy Perkins lock, stock and barrel; the new owners quickly parted company with the Think Tank who were never seen again.

Over the past six years I had lived at a very fast pace. Mentally I could remember coping with a million details. Physically I could bound up five flights of stairs of the Big Biba without a puff. Home had become just a dosshouse. Suddenly I was trapped in my home. I found it difficult to wind down to this pace. I would worry for hours about a hole that had appeared in the sheets or a cup whose handle had broken off. There were towels that were worn out and I was faced with making a major decision about whether to continue with the same colour or branch out to another one.

I couldn't cope with minor personal problems. I had never had time to develop my own personality. I still didn't know who I was and didn't particularly want to, either. When you have had a million people and things to worry about, suddenly to find yourself faced with just you is a shock to the system. I was even feeling out of step with Fitz's problems, although they were really my problems too. I would begin the day worrying about which cupboard I should start clearing, but the whole day would pass without my having even started. While I sat at home Fitz would always hold back all the bad bits from me. He felt there was no need for me to know.

In the past I sometimes imagined that someone had come and taken Biba away from me. After it happened and Biba was no longer mine I once came across a Biba cosmetics stand in Paris at a Prêt à Porter show. The stand looked awful and I longed to go and tidy it up for them. They had put the colours out all wrong. The man on the stand wore gold chains around his neck, his shirt undone to his navel. The sales girls looked cheap and tarty. They were trying to imitate Biba but had got it all wrong, and there was nothing I could do about it except walk away. It really hurt. I still feel it today. I want to go up to Biba cosmetics counters and smash every pot of make-up there.

During this difficult time I found it very hard to talk to my mother. I knew she felt sorry for me but it was the last thing I needed. At that moment I knew what was on her lips – 'You shouldn't have started it' – and I didn't know if I could keep myself under control.

Finally British Land decided that they and their acolytes could no longer run the store. They decided to auction off the entire interior. Fitz and I were amazed at the interest of both private collectors and museums. Later the assistant curator of the Museum of Modern Art in New York told me how sad he had been that he had no money left at the time to buy anything for the museum. Oddly it cheered us tremendously to think that so many of our things would find a good home where they would be appreciated. Unfortunately this was not always the case. After the auction it hurt to see part of Biba in tacky shops down the Earls Court Road. The fibreglass Othello had disappeared. They wouldn't let me buy it. I don't know why. It was a personal statement. He had just died and I would have liked his towering effigy, with a fig leaf covering his private parts, at home. It had disappeared from the loading bay and everyone had assumed Fitz and I had bought him, but it was never seen again.

I was in limbo. I had never been free to do so many things. Maybe now I could do something worthwhile, help in a home for unwanted children or maybe visit old people. Yet I sat there and did nothing. For the last eight months I had waited daily for something to happen. In the evenings I would wait for Fitz to come home. I wanted him to come through the door with that grin from one ear to the other as he had in the pink gingham days in Golden Square. He always tried to look happy when he came home, but I could tell it was just a very noble effort made for me.

If I didn't get up with Fitz I would just stay in my night clothes all day. Witold had his busy life downstairs. I didn't fit into his routine: tea parties with other children, walks in the park, and television. The only thing that still interested me and gave me an escape was movies. I tried to make up for all the films I had missed in the last eight years. I would try and see three a day. If I timed it right I could just manage to get to three cinemas, starting at midday, charging from the Paris Pullman across London to the Academy 1 and 2 in Oxford Street.

My friends all worked. Sometimes Cilla Black, Cathy McGowan or Twiggy and I would have lunch together, but I felt so left out without a job to do. One lunchtime I was at Lorenzo's waiting for Twiggy to arrive. Most people in the room had a job to go to, a desk to sit behind. The others led a life of endless lunches and self-imposed chores. That was not the life for me.

Of the other people that had started with us in the original shop in 1964, Elly, who became the senior manager after Sarah, was with us to the bitter end. Irene had become unwell in 1968 in our first shop on the High Street, then married, and was now living in Iran. Kim, who had also left about this time, although I forget why, telephoned us out of the blue when she heard the bad news and asked if she could work for us without pay. It was a touching and moving gesture. An Irish former maintenance man asked if we would like him to blow up the building for us – no, please don't, we begged. Now here was Sarah. Many years had gone by but it was as if she had never been away. We just continued our conversation where we left off. I missed Rosie. She and Sarah were Witold's godmothers. Sarah said I should see Rosie again. She was now married to Tony, who had also worked for us in the old days and had left when they started their own business. We had gradually grown apart and she now had three children. It seemed so many years had been wasted.

Now, when the chips were down, many old friends made contact again.

Should I have listened to Fitz – should we have stopped when British Land took us over? What would have happened to Biba? Would it just have come to a less spectacular end much sooner? I believed we could have beaten it. We always could move mountains, and we had our share of bad luck. The day we put out our first mail-order catalogue there was a postal strike. When we opened the Big Biba we were up against the three-day week. But if Ritblat had not preferred to lease the building to Marks & Spencer and British Home Stores I believe we would have pulled through. I really believe that there was too much life and energy and goodwill within Biba for it to die. Big Biba was a dinosaur that moved slowly, and after perfecting things it would take a while for results to be apparent. If you keep correcting, things will suddenly start straightening themselves out. What was Harrods like on its opening day?

If you opened a big store today you would have no staff problems. People would be happy to have work. When Biba opened it was a problem to keep shop staff, who by nature were gypsies and would wander off. The special ones stayed on because they could see a future.

Meanwhile, Fitz was trying to save Biba and was still in the big store. It had become obvious that it was impossible for us to buy the building, but Fitz had found a man who controlled a small public company and who wanted to be our partner. We negotiated with British Land to buy the thriving cosmetics company and all the Biba trademarks. The price was agreed and our new partners were ready with their money.

We had new premises earmarked and we were waiting for the contracts to be prepared, but our relationship with Roxburgh had now reached a state when it seemed to us that he would do anything to spite us. He would send chauffeurs round to our house with legal documents for us to sign there and then. He would write us memos, which seemed to us to be so complicated legally that we had to ask our solicitor to respond, and it always had to be done with unusual [...] Fitz heard the rumour that British Land were negotiating with [...] company at Ritblat's office. A lightning board meeting was called and it was announced that they had sold Biba Cosmetics and trademarks to a financier called Dobson, who was frontman for another property company. Roxburgh was furious that I was not at that meeting. He moved a formal motion that I should be censored for not being present but I had no wish to give him the satisfaction of seeing me as he finally sold Biba.

Fitz rang me. 'We've lost,' he said. 'I'm coming home.'

The relief was immense. We were free again. As Fitz came through the door I could tell that he felt the same way I did. There was a grin on his face. 'Thank God that's over,' he said.

Our day was made when Mr Dobson, the proud new owner of the Biba name, rang us up to ask when we were going to start work. He really thought that he had bought us along with the company. In so many words I told him to get stuffed. Everybody thought that it was easy – that the image was so strong it would last for ever. They did not realize that Biba was a being that changed from day to day, needing care and protection. It could not be sealed in a time capsule or exploited by people who did not understand it. Everybody since who has tried to cash in on the Biba name has failed completely. They have not realized that the name in itself means nothing. It is only as strong as the idea it evokes in the minds of other people. Biba was a very delicate balance, achieved by all of those directly involved and the public. No amount of promotion or commercialization can replace the genuine article.

'I have a great idea,' said Fitz. 'Let's go to Brazil.'

We were so lucky to have each other and Witold, and could re-establish our family relationships. Witold had never had a full-time mum and dad. We were leaving home and many heartaches but our new life was tackling the unknown. We knew no one and we hoped no one knew Biba. We had to get to know each other again – get back to square one.

While we were waiting for our Brazilian papers we had thrown so many goodbye parties that everyone thought we would never actually go away. I couldn't get myself to begin packing. When our visas came, in May 1976, we had to start. Half-heartedly we put the studio up for sale and Rosie and Tony took our packed crates into their new empty house until it was time to despatch them to the banana boat. We had left the giant mirrors and big pieces of furniture in the studio. I secretly hoped the house wouldn't ever sell, even though we were supposed to be going, never to return.

Funnily enough, for ages the house wasn't sold, but invaded by squatters. A couple of them happened to be old Biba girls and their boyfriends. When we reached Brazil we received messages from the squatters: 'Not to worry – we are paying the gas and electricity bills.' This was very comforting! The gallery in the studio was now draped in swastikas and all day the stereos thumped out recordings of Hitler's speeches at the highest pitch. We telephoned Rosie and Tony, who said he was going in there to get the rest of the jumbo mirrors and the furniture. The following week Tony and Rosie sent us a cutting from the *Evening Standard*. The headline was, 'Barbara Hulanicki Flat Raided'. The squatters had notified the police that a gang of heavies had come and stolen our furniture. Tony and his building team had gone in there and removed anything that was destructible and of any value. The saga lifted our spirits a bit. It was a relief during homesick days in Brazil. When eventually the house *was* sold, all links with England were broken, and we had no excuse left to return.

As I roamed round London taking a last look, it was full of ex-Biba girls. In Biba they were always free to air their views to me. They would tell me what was selling, what was wrongly displayed, what was impractical to get at. In 1976 if I met any Biba girl working in another shop they would automatically tell me all their work problems. I was touched but I had to explain that it wasn't my shop. I would go to Way In at Harrods to see the Biba cosmetics counter. The girl behind the unit asked me to put the display right as they had made her change it all round. It didn't work as far as she was concerned and it did look awful, but I stood there helpless; there was nothing I could do. I once went to Debenhams to buy a Biba cream powder tint. The girl was a stranger to me. She said 'We don't make cream colour powder.'

'Yes you do, look under the counter,' I said.

More annoying were girls who had only just started working for the new cosmetics company and who would give me a hard sell spiel – often their information was all wrong and the heartless hard sell was enough to make anybody run away. How could cosmetics be run by a committee of businessmen? They didn't know what women wanted.

When we finally had Biba taken from us we were left with nothing, and as they say, we soon learned who our friends were. Some dropped you immediately, others started dreaming of imaginary debts, trying to milk us for the last possible drop. Presidents of American stores who had been friends for years were suddenly out when we rang. I must say that the press and TV journalists here were terrific. They were all on our side and the coverage that they gave us was really fair. Among the most memorable was an article called 'The Battle for Biba', by Philip Norman of the *Sunday Times* colour magazine. Philip came to do 'a day in the life of' story and stayed off and on for six months, recording the ridiculous doings, moves and counter moves of our partners. I think he summed everything up when he wrote 'in early days at Biba they used to sell dog ornaments with nodding heads as a joke. At the end nodding-headed dogs were sold at Biba in earnest.' Another marvellous piece was by Frankie McGowan in the *Evening News*. 'Biba Boss Speaks Out' was on the placards that day, and Frankie really captured the frustration and incredulity that we felt. The first time I started to hear nice things about Biba was after we closed. I thought the press would be pleased the shop was closed, but now I heard nothing but praise, which baffled me. If I had been more secure I would never have taken any notice of the moans. You learn that people never tell you anything nice – you only hear the bad things. Now our house was bombarded with telephone calls day and night.

We were inundated by lunatic proposals. Two theatrical agents approached us with an idea for opening franchise shops all over the world. They claimed that they had become friendly with a number of eastern princesses. From Ceylon via Singapore to the Middle East their connections were endless. The first time they came to see us they were dressed in bowlers and pinstripes with wing collars. The second time they arrived in kaftans over their formal clothes. One had an enormous bow tie and both were playing with worry beads. We named them Og and Mogg and their grandiose ideas kept us in stitches. Our last conversation with them took place late on the night before we went off to Brazil. When the phone rang Fitz was asleep. He grunted hello and sat as if mesmerized, listening to the voice at the other end. After a long one-sided conversation, he put the telephone back and turned to me with a bemused look.

'It's Og and Mogg,' he said. 'It's all changed. They are going to make a film of your life. They say that you can play yourself, but I can't. They want to know if you'd mind if Warren Beatty played me.'

We looked at each other, speechless, and went back to sleep.

A particularly unsavoury man had been calling us from America. He was in the cosmetics business and we knew that he had robbed one of our competitors of a large amount. He was frantic to get hold of us and kept on getting Witold on the other end of the line. One Sunday we were having a lunch party when the phone rang. Witold, who was eight, answered the call and was talking away to what we assumed was a friend. He then went over to Fitz and said that there was someone who wanted to speak to him. At that moment the front doorbell rang and Fitz went to open it, forgetting all about the phone. A good twenty minutes later he noticed that the phone was off the hook. He went to put it back and in passing said hello to the receiver. Hello, hello, came the reply. It was the man from New York.

'I wanna put Biba on the map,' he said. He was a month too late.

In 1971, on one of her regular cruises, my aunt had decided to marry again. The lucky man was head steward on board ship. Basil was very tall and distinguished looking, fifteen years her junior. After the wedding he took Auntie's last name and became Basil Gassner. Although Mother had been married to Humphrey for eighteen years, she found a void without my aunt's constant reprimands. From her childhood she had been conditioned to seek the approval of my aunt for the smallest thing. Apart from her few years with my father, Auntie had been the cornerstone of her life, but now Auntie was completely engrossed in another world.

I hadn't seen Auntie since my sister Biba's wedding in 1963, and dearly wanted to contact her after so long. Mother had always told me that my aunt never wanted to speak to me again as long as she lived, but when the Big Biba opened I plucked up courage and sent her a Biba diary for 1974 with a note. Surely I was now an equal? One evening the telephone rang – it was Basil. He said, 'Aunt Sophie wants to thank you for the present.' Then Auntie came on the telephone and said how lovely the diary was and how pleased she was I had done something positive with my life.

I couldn't speak. I just cried. I had not seen her for eleven years. I now wanted so much to see her again. She went on speaking and then abruptly stopped. Basil came on the line again and said he wanted to see Auntie and me get together, and she wanted it too. Basil had apparently been trying to bridge the rift between us for three years. I was about to go to Milan, and he promised to arrange a meeting when I got back. On my second night in Milan, Fitz telephoned and told me that she was dead.

I had never realized before how much she meant to me and how much she had affected everything in my life and thinking. Maybe she did love me. After everything that I had done, even now, I automatically thought, 'What would Auntie say?'

I cried the whole night. My ambivalent feelings had just turned to love for her. I wish I hadn't been too proud to seek her out, but I had such resentments. I also feared that Auntie might think I was after her money. She always accused everybody of this and she was usually right. Years earlier my aunt had made a trust for my mother: on my mother's death the money was to go to my two sisters. I did not know that at my sister Biba's wedding, the first and only time Auntie had met Fitz, Auntie had liked him and changed the trust to include me. Auntie had refused to acknowledge my presence and I was banished to a table of acquaintances and former employees. Fitz, however, was seated at her right hand to be inspected and adjudged. Fitz found her stream of insults and commands, directed at those around her in a growling Marlene Dietrich accent, one of the classic comic episodes of his life, and could not see why she had such a stranglehold on my life. They were soon quaffing wine and talking animatedly about a recent exhibition of Spanish painters, a subject about which neither of them knew anything at all. By the time she had exhorted a leading dignitary of the Polish movement in exile, who was giving a speech, to 'Get on with it, you old fool', Fitz was nearly crying with laughter and the two of them parted, somewhat unsteadily, with mutual expressions of pleasure at their encounter.

My aunt had thoroughly approved of Fitz, particularly after she had found out that his surname was not derived from the English bastard line but was of the Norman Irish variety.

The day after Auntie died, Fitz and Witold flew to Milan to be with me. I felt shattered, filled with quiet and remorse. My aunt *was* Biba. I hadn't really understood till now, but she had been my inspiration. It was her sense of colour, her love for grandeur, the nostalgia of her glorious youth – all the things that I had hated about her when I was very young. I wish there had been some communication between us. If only she had allowed a little freedom of thought maybe I wouldn't have fought her so hard.

My aunt's funeral was a fiasco. My mother was on the verge of hysteria because it was held in a non-Catholic church and, worse, my aunt was to be cremated. To Mother, a devout Catholic, this meant Auntie would be doomed to eternal hell. Basil had instructed no flowers. I thought damn it, and sent a huge pink heart from Witold, whom she had never met. This upset my mother further, since she hadn't the nerve to go against Basil's wishes. Before the service the priest asked my mother if Auntie was a good woman! My mother nearly thumped him. Of course she was a wonderful woman. She paid for everything!

Throughout the ceremony my poor mother kept up a monologue accusing Basil of drowning my aunt in gin and of never really having loved her. As the coffin slid down the ramp, Basil threw himself across it, and in a voice shaking with melodramatic emotion he professed his eternal love for Sophie and started to slip towards the doors of the crematorium. Mother stopped her tirade as we all watched Basil's progress and then rescue. It was difficult to continue weeping after that!

The year after my aunt died we went to Brighton for the weekend. As usual I went round the antique shops. In one of them I found her initialled ermine neck scarf hanging amongst a lot of old clothes. I couldn't bring myself to buy it.

Auntie had died the day her money ran out. It was almost as if she had paced her life to the last moment and then turned the switch off. In control as usual. I think that old people die not always because their bodies have ceased to function but because they are not wanted any more, or because they have done their stretch on earth and are ready for better times.

In 1979, when my mother was dying, I asked the priest why she was suffering so much. Her 'suffering' was our penance. She was now on another plane, preparing herself for a new life. She went away very slowly and very serenely after the priest left. After she had gone I sat with her for a long time. She looked very beautiful. All the troubled wrinkles had been smoothed away. She had waited for me to get back from Brazil where I was then living. She was in a complete coma but during the night I was left alone with her. She opened her eyes and her dilated pupils came to life for a moment to give me a sign that she knew I was there. We were saying goodbye. The first time I really believed in God and beyond was when I saw the shell of my dead mother. The spirit had flown away, and oddly it was a very happy moment. The body was just a picture frame for the lovely soul. The sorrow and pain were mine, not hers. She was now completely happy with her loved ones again, in another timespan. I was there with her, and so were my father, my sisters and my aunt. We lived happily ever after.

On the journey to Heathrow Airport the little rows and rows of grey houses, similiar to those that had looked so hostile twenty-six years ago when we arrived from Palestine, now looked friendly and comforting. Their gardens were filled with flowers and blossom-covered trees. Plastic red-hatted gnomes had come out to wait hopefully for the coming summer. I don't think we were aware what a big decision we had taken until the taxi driver drew up at Terminal Three. We each had the regulation 20 kilos of luggage and the three of us carried hand luggage that weighed at least as much again. Witold, now eight, was struggling with a holdall of his precious *Marvel* comics. His little face was turning blue but we had made a pact before leaving that any personal possessions had to be handled by their owner. We were to travel light – I suppose it *was* light considering there would be no return journey. These were our belongings for the new life we were to embark on in Brazil. Fitz asked me if I was sure I wanted to go, there was still time to turn back – 'No, we must go on.' It was either this or a life of perpetual nostalgia.

As we checked our luggage in, the tannoy was calling for Mr and Mrs Fitz-Simon. Had something happened? Was there an eleventh-hour reprieve? When we found the telephone, Michael Whitney and Twiggy were wishing us luck. Now I was weeping, Witold was looking at me with surprise. He couldn't understand the tears. Weren't we going for a very long holiday? It was then I realized that, after all those years of considering myself a refugee, this was home, and I was leaving it.

Epilogue

After Biba closed in September 1975, Fitz, Witold and I went to lick our wounds in far away Brazil. Carmen Miranda was calling. We had both been battered by the fight to retain the Biba name but had lost the name and our identity.

Everywhere we went there was a pirate Biba store. In sunny, sticky Rio we threw ourselves into an exciting new life, not understanding a word of Portuguese. We manufactured in Sao Paolo and travelled to Europe with special collections for Cacharel and the vibrating Fiorucci. Eventually it was time for Witold to go to school in England and so we followed him back home.

By chance I was asked to design a club for Ronnie Wood, the first rock 'n' roll club in the decaying Art Deco beach town in Miami. Fitz, meanwhile, was in bliss writing books and stories which never reached a publisher but then together we wrote a Milli Vanilli novel, *Disgrace*, based on *From A to Biba*, which was actually published!

On the beach I met Chris Blackwell, the founder of Island Records, who owned a derelict building in Miami called the Marlin. He asked if I would like to work on it and the Marlin became the first boutique hotel, a hub of rock star parties and fun, rather reminiscent of the early sixties in London.

16 years later, we were still on the beach. We had worked on nine of the − then unappreciated − magnificent tropical Deco buildings, sometimes three times over as Chris had bought a job lot of them. My projects, designing the hotels, had the same rhythm of stress as the schmata trade − not helped by the fact that I had to marry Jamaican with tropical Deco style. This time I was fighting plumbers and electricians: a change from East End dress manufacturers. Simultaneously I worked for Gloria and Emilio Estefan, designing their enormous home on Star Island in Miami, as well as designing costumes with a Cuban flavour for one of Gloria's videos. Later, Chris Blackwell asked me to design the interiors for Golden Eye in Jamaica. It was Ian Fleming's home where he wrote the Bond novels. The development project is still ongoing. . .

New Bibas came and went without our involvement. Although very painful to me, Fitz would always turn it into a laugh. We would bet how long they would last. Much money was lost by these upstart pretenders. The original Biba had never lost money, another joke to us. None of the new holders of the Biba licence could understand the magic of the period, the essence of camaraderie among the young. It was instigated by the young and for the young and now the dolly dress was dead.

London today is once again the most exciting, creative city and Biba babies are in charge all over the place. 12 years before Fitz died he encouraged me to go back to illustration. He thought it was time for me to move from building sites and eventually I did. I was asked to design bags for Coccinelle in Italy, wallpaper for Habitat and Graham & Brown, and draw illustrations for Manny Mashouf at Bebe in LA.

In 2008, Oberon Sinclair pushed me to put on a show of my drawings at Andrew Coningsby's Gallery in London. Sam Summerskill in turn then introduced me to Charlotte Henson at Topshop, whom I went on to design a range of clothes for in spring/summer 2009. So here I am, back to where I started, worrying about all those crooked seams and wobbly hems!

Barbara Hulanicki
Miami   2009